PRAISE FOR **THE VIRTUAL MANAGER**

"This lucid and concise book contains much common sense about the realities of managing colleagues you cannot see. Sheridan reminds us that some timeless human virtues—the ability to listen, to empathize, to communicate clearly—are needed in the modern globalized corporation as much as (and perhaps more than) ever."

—Stefan Stern, director of strategy at Edelman in London, visiting professor of management practice at Cass Business School

"This insightful book contains actionable advice and fascinating case studies that will help managers effectively manage, empower, and engage their virtual workers. Kevin Sheridan's best practices for motivating and engaging the virtual workforce are both thought-provoking and illuminating."

—David Shadovitz, editor of *Human Resource Executive*

"A passionate evidence-based argument for why virtual working not only improves performance through active employee engagement but also makes better use of time, reduces absence levels, and is also good for the environment."

—Mick Marchington, professor of Human Resource Management at Manchester Business School and coauthor of *Fragmenting Work*

"This insightful book recognizes that 'work' is not a place, but instead it's the act of value creation that can happen anytime and anywhere. With this shift comes the need for a new set of guidelines, skills, and resources, not just for individuals and teams, but for their managers too. **The Virtual Manager** is packed full of smart ideas that leaders can use to build an effective and engaged virtual workforce, and leverage all the benefits that remote working has to offer."

—Jennifer Rosenzweig, research director, The Forum: Business Results Through People, affiliated with Northwestern University

CUTTING-EDGE SOLUTIONS FOR HIRING, MANAGING, MOTIVATING, AND ENGAGING MOBILE EMPLOYEES

THE VIRTUAL MANAGER

KEVIN SHERIDAN

Pompton Plains, N.J.

The Virtual Manager
Edited and Typeset by Kara Kumpel
Cover design by Ty Nowicki
Printed in the U.S.A.

To order this title, please call toll-free 1-800-CAREER-1 (NJ and Canada: 201-848-0310) to order using VISA or MasterCard, or for further information on books from Career Press.

The Career Press, Inc.
220 West Parkway, Unit 12
Pompton Plains, NJ 07444
www.careerpress.com

Library of Congress Cataloging-in-Publication Data

Sheridan, Kevin, 1960-
The virtual manager : cutting-edge solutions for hiring, managing, motivating, and engaging mobile employees / Kevin Sheridan. -- 1
p. cm.
Includes bibliographical references and index.
ISBN 978-1-60163-185-5 (pbk.)
1. Telecommuting--Management. 2. Virtual work teams--Management. 3. Employee motivation. 4. Organizational effectiveness. I. Title.
HD2336.3.S54 2012
658.3'123--dc23

2011043023

I want to dedicate this book to the millions of virtual employees and virtual managers around our globe, who both struggle and succeed in bridging the management and human gulf between each other; the very genesis for this book was to help in that meaningful purpose. I look forward to and invite hearing about your success stories after implementing the best practices discussed in the book.

Yours Virtually,

Kevin

ACKNOWLEDGMENTS

I give incredibly heartfelt thanks, praise, and recognition (a key Driver of Engagement featured in Chapter 4) to the many HR Solutions marketing team members who made this book possible: Ashley Nuese, Kristina Anderson, Michael Savitt, Melissa Herrett, Amelia Forczak, and Lisa Henthorn; these talented individuals are certainly helping me to think as, and aspire to become, a great virtual manager.

Deep thanks to my wife, Barb, and my two young daughters, Morgan and Hannah, for their love and support while I was oftentimes very virtual, writing this book somewhere other than home.

Special thanks to Maryann Karinch, who was instrumental in making this project a reality.

Lastly, some of the most pertinent best practices in this book came from the many employees at HR Solutions, who have consistently taught their senior leaders the important best practices of letting go and building trust.

CONTENTS

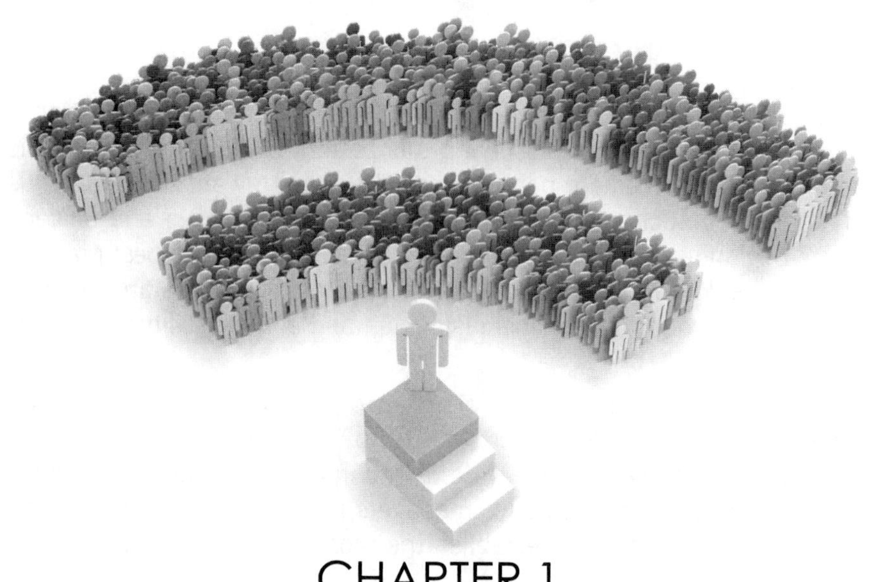

CHAPTER 1

A NEW WAY OF DOING BUSINESS: VIRTUAL TEAMS

Business, more than any other occupation, is a continual dealing with the future; it is a continual calculation, an instinctive exercise in foresight.

—Henry R. Luce, author

When organizations look to the future, the most innovative and successful leaders realize the potential that virtual workforces have to change the face of business. Increasingly, leadership and organizations are viewing "work" as something you do, rather than somewhere you go. As organizations expand across the nation and the globe, remote labor forces are becoming vital to business success. Currently, 82 percent of *Fortune Magazine*'s "100 Best Companies to Work For" already have virtual work policies. That number is expected to rise as time and technology advance.

As working at a distance continues to take root, virtual workplaces may soon become more common than physical office spaces,[1] especially when you factor in the past growth rate. Each year, the population of virtual workers grows, and observing this pattern contributes to the belief that virtual workforces are here to stay. The trend toward virtual work is, in fact, gaining such a hold in the workplace that colleges and universities are beginning to introduce programs dedicated solely to best practices for virtual work. To remain up to par in this increasingly distanced world, managers must consider the increasing demand and necessity for a virtual workforce.

Remote workforces help maintain an organization's competitive advantage. Distance employees contribute to higher profits, larger market shares, and an ambitious edge. Prior to incorporating remote workers into your organization, it is imperative managers understand every facet of the virtual workforce in order to establish the most successful virtual teams.

WHAT IS A VIRTUAL WORKER?

Virtual work has not always looked the same. Remote jobs were originally referred to as *telecommuting*, reflecting the most commonly perceived benefit of such work: reduced commute times. As employers began to view telecommuting as benefitting more than just commuters, *telework* was adopted as a broader term. The most recent phrase, *virtual work*, is an all-encompassing term meant to refer to entire populations who are working together, separately. For the purposes of this book, I will be all-inclusive in my definition: A *virtual employee* is anyone who works remotely or in a different location than her manager or peers. A *virtual manager* is a leader who manages employees in various locales.

Whether referred to as *telecommuting*, *teleworking*, or *working virtually*, there are multiple types of virtual employees. Currently, the remote population ranges from 15 to 30 million people, based on a five-year study of trends in distance working.[2] The large range is due to these varying definitions of virtual workers:

- An employee who regularly meets with clients at his place of business, rarely or never working from his own office or home.
- A team member who works from home, a coffee shop, library, or wherever she chooses.
- A person with coworkers in various other locations.
- A leader in the corporate office who manages employees across the globe.

Further complicating the meaning of *virtual employee*, definitions vary by frequency. Some virtual workers are considered remote employees because they work outside of the office one day a year; others work virtually every day. Here are a few more definitions:

- A worker who schedules clients Monday through Thursday and catches up on work from a remote location on Fridays.
- An individual who works at a distance only once or twice a year.
- An employee who is permitted to work wherever he chooses twice each quarter.

Working remotely can take multiple forms, and it is important to recognize how varied the practice is. Each of the aforementioned individuals is a virtual worker in the broadest definition of the term, and this list is in no way all-inclusive. Every type of virtual worker brings a unique perspective to the table. Additionally, each category requires various tailored practices in order to be the most successful.

With the transition of "work" from "somewhere you go" to "something you do," virtual work is impossible to ignore any longer. Remote employees will continue to play a role in changing organizations across the world. As an effective manager, you need to be prepared to incorporate the changing business environment into your organization. This book will provide you with vital tools and best practices to implement the most effective virtual workforce, allowing you to create the most successful organization.

WHEN IS A VIRTUAL STAFF THE BEST OPTION?

The answer is simple: when you want greater business success. Often, virtual work is not an *option*, but a *necessity* to gain market share. Global organizations are able to provide better service and ultimately a better product when employees live near clients and customers and fully understand their needs. Having a team of remote and virtual employees is a great fit for global business because everyone benefits: employees, clients, and the company as a whole. Employees enjoy the perk of added flexibility, while clients and customers are able to work with local employees anywhere across the globe. In addition, the organization benefits because it is able to recruit from around the world, allowing it to hire some of the most talented people in the industry.

Whether your organization establishes virtual teams in order to meet clients on-site, or to reach a wider customer base and gain a competitive advantage, remote employees will have an impact on your organization. Virtual workforces are the future, and they are your best option for the greatest business success.

Currently, some managers may view remote teams as a thorn in the side of talent management. They recognize some of the benefits, but still feel the risks are too great to truly implement a valuable virtual workforce. Although they realize the advantages virtual employees could provide, many managers worry about regulation, productivity, and other challenges. However, virtual teams may be more advantageous than managers realize. It is imperative leadership understands both the benefits and drawbacks of a virtual workforce in depth, prior to implementing any virtual work policies. Thoroughly examining both the pros and cons of remote teams will be critical to creating the most successful virtual workforce, one that will provide higher profits, a more diverse customer base, a higher ROI, and greater employee engagement.

The reasons many employees would prefer to work virtually may be easily recognizable: greater work/life balance, more autonomy, and less money spent on gas, to name a few. Although the direct benefits for employers are not so evident, remote workforces can actually contribute to a higher ROI in various ways. It is fundamental to explore each beneficial facet of working at a distance to truly understand the impact virtual employees can have on an organization.

ATTRACTING TOP TALENT

Virtual work policies can be used to maintain a competitive advantage, drawing highly skilled individuals to your organization. The most successful businesses are built on a foundation of top talent who contribute to positive organizational outcomes. Exceptional employees afford higher profits, greater productivity, and increased market share. Thus, remote work policies can serve as magnetic attractors to draw top talent to your organization.

Flexible work policies attract employees. Talented workers are in high demand, often receiving multiple job offers in a short period of time. A virtual work policy will encourage skilled professionals to join an organization's team. In one study of hiring managers and workers across various industries and organizations, a large majority of employees, 72 percent, stated flexible work arrangements would cause them to choose one job over another, and 37 percent of this majority cited working virtually specifically.[3] Additionally, employees are so drawn to virtual work that they are willing to give up items such as their favorite TV show (54 percent), an extra hour of sleep (48 percent), and a portion of their salary (40 percent).[4] Organizations that implement virtual work policies will thus have a competitive advantage in hiring. One best practice to attract top talent is to tout the fact that an organization has a virtual work policy and flexible hours directly in the offer letter. Employees will then be aware of this option, thus possibly contributing to a higher likelihood that they will accept the job.

Distance working provides a greater personal and professional balance, which is another key selling point for employees. As Baby Boomers mature and retire, and younger generations canvas the workforce, many employees are replacing the "living to work" mentality with a "working to live" attitude. "Working to live" often takes the form of a work/life balance. Younger generations tend to value organizations that allow them time for activities and personal lives outside of their jobs. Virtual work policies give employees more flexible schedules, as well as time to manage personal obligations, thus increasing the feelings of balance. This balance is a huge draw, attracting top talent dedicated to balancing work and life.

In addition to attracting the best workers for the job, remote work policies also provide employers with access to a wider hiring pool, thereby increasing their chances of finding the most qualified individuals for their organization. Managers can hire individuals from across the world without worrying about relocation, and employees in various locations can consider opportunities in other locales without having to move. Personal connections such as the desire to stay in a certain school district, wanting to remain close to family, or lack of funds to relocate often limit the potential job opportunities available; virtual work policies mitigate this issue. Attracting top talent from various locales contributes to greater diversity, more varied viewpoints, and a more well-rounded organization as a whole. As diversity within an organization attracts more workers, establishing a culture filled with various individuals from different backgrounds will contribute magnetic attractors to your organization as well. Thus, not only will you attract top talent from various locales, but you will also establish a culture that in itself attracts more skilled individuals.

Virtual managers can also utilize their engaged employees, both on-site and virtually, to attract top talent. Top-talent virtual employees in search of job opportunities can bridge the distance during their job hunt by contacting a company's previous employees through social media to better understand the organization's culture prior to applying. For example, before becoming an indispensible member of our team, one employee at HR Solutions searched previous employees on LinkedIn and asked them for a reference, so she could have a more comprehensive view of the organization. Upon acquiring this information, she decided she would be a good fit, and the rest is history. Without ever meeting anyone face-to-face prior to the interview, this employee was able to understand the culture, and was attracted to the organization. Virtual managers would thus do well to follow this example and create a culture of attraction built on top talent.

RETAINING TOP TALENT

Remote workers have a 60 percent higher intent to stay than employees in a traditional office setting.[5] Because of this, employers should establish a virtual work policy in order to retain their best team members. It costs less to retain employees than it does to train new hires, with training and hiring costs amounting to 150 to 200 percent of an individual's salary.[6] The bottom line is reduced, and greater business success results from retaining top talent.

One reason many employees choose to leave their jobs is burnout, which results from team members becoming overburdened and disillusioned, either from too much work or from not accomplishing their desired goals. But employees who work virtually are less likely to get burnt out from their jobs. According to one study conducted at Brigham Young University, virtual workers and flextime employees work an additional 19 hours (more than two days!) per week before feeling overwhelmed.[7] The ability to work additional hours is likely due to a greater work/life balance and the reduction in stress that results from working virtually. With remote work strategies in place, employees are less likely to feel overloaded and thus are more likely to remain with an organization.

The reduction in stress afforded by remote work policies contributes to retention beyond burnout as well. A large cause of stress among employees is attributed to commuter stress, which can be greatly reduced or completely eliminated with the establishment of virtual work policies.

According to research by David Lewis, commuters actually experience more stress than policemen and fighter pilots.[8] Doesn't that seem a bit extreme? These high levels of stress are largely attributed to the lack of control commuters have over their circumstances. I know I've left the house many days with plenty of time to spare, only to arrive 15 minutes late to work because of traffic, something I cannot control. Even disregarding lateness, employees may not have time to decompress before they have to jump right into work following a stressful commute. Frustration from commuting often carries over into the workplace, affecting productivity, interactions with coworkers and management, and positive feelings about the organization and an employee's job.

Remote work policies also contribute to retention through the reduction in forced turnover. By this I do not mean termination; rather, I am referring to those employees who would like to remain at a job, but due to personal obligations, must resign. When virtual work policies are established, individuals can stay with an aging parent or child recovering from surgery and still contribute to their job duties. They do not have to quit working in order to do so. As the number of individuals with caregiving responsibilities is increasing,[9] managers would do well to implement virtual work policies to retain talented employees who would otherwise need to leave. Allowing employees to work outside the office will contribute to a balance between personal caregiving responsibilities and job obligations.

Talented employees who must move out of state for various reasons can also be retained if allowed to work virtually. Consider a skilled employee whose wife just obtained her dream job in another state. A virtual work policy would allow this employee to remain with his organization while still allowing his wife to do what she loves. Additionally, the organization benefits from retaining a highly skilled and dedicated employee who puts forth discretionary effort for better business outcomes. Virtual work policies are a win-win in these situations: Employers are able to retain not just top talent, but *proven* talent that produces great work, as these employees have shown themselves to be beneficial and engaged in the organization. More than 59 percent of employees who leave an organization do so within six months to a year, and of those who stay, another 50 percent leave before two years of employment. Thus, 79.5 percent of your employees never make it beyond the two-year mark.[10] Virtual managers will benefit greatly from retaining those employees they know are already invested, dedicated, and in it for the long haul.

Workplace flexibility also allows organizations to retain top talent by avoiding the "Brain Drain" effect, which occurs when a large cohort of skilled individuals leaves a location for a multitude of reasons. For example, as Baby Boomers reach retirement, the skills and knowledge these individuals offer will be removed in a short period of time. The effects of a mass exodus could be reduced through remote work possibilities. Indeed, 75 percent of retirees would prefer to continue to work, but want the flexibility that can be offered through virtual work policies.[11] Allowing employees to work remotely will lessen the impact when individuals within a generation retire at similar times.

Virtual managers can thus leverage distance working to retain the employees they do not want to lose.

THE BOTTOM-LINE BENEFITS OF VIRTUAL EMPLOYEES

A More Satisfied and Varied Customer Base

Virtual employees working in remote locations can offer insight on various cultures, contributing to a better understanding of the many wants and desires of customers around the world. In this way, remote workers can be viewed as untapped resources of market research. After all, team members across the globe likely know more about what is happening in their local culture than managers in a different location, and, as such, are more able to determine what products are most successful, how products are best branded, and so on. Employees working directly with customers are more knowledgeable and able to understand the customers' desires and needs.

Additionally, virtual employees are advantageous for continuous customer service and progress: When organizations have locations in different time zones all over the world, customers will likely always be able to reach an employee because a team member will always be working somewhere. Progress is being made around the clock as well: Organizations that institute a virtual work policy can remain competitive globally by providing exceptional customer service 24 hours a day.

Fewer Overhead Costs

One of the biggest advantages managers see when implementing a virtual workforce is the reduction in costs otherwise assumed to be standard. For example, the cost of office space for the average worker is estimated to be $10,000 a year.[12] This dollar amount includes real estate, office supplies, furniture, Internet and phone lines, and other expenses associated with working in an office. But when employees work virtually, they do not necessarily need individual work stations. Desks, chairs, phones, and other supplies do not need to be purchased by employers, thus reducing overhead costs. Building security and maintenance fees can also be cut to save additional funds.

Even if employers choose to cover a portion of the expenses needed for virtual work stations, the overhead cost is still much less than if employers supply an actual physical space for team members. Organizations are able to save on real estate as well. IBM, for instance, has saved $700 million a year in real estate costs by allowing 25 percent of their employees to work from a distance. With 80,000 of their 320,000 workers working virtually, the computer manufacturer is able to reduce the number of offices required for all of its team members.[13] Following this example, leadership of virtual teams can purchase smaller office buildings, cutting costs dramatically. The overhead for expenses is generally much less than covering an actual physical space with amenities.

With a reduction in the required office space, employers also save on energy costs. As seasons change, organizations reduce their costs on heating and air conditioning bills when spaces are smaller. Energy costs are often a huge investment by employers, and switching to a greater percentage of virtual workers would reduce the cost of lighting offices, running refrigerators, powering microwaves in the kitchen, operating water coolers, and many other bills employers often assume are unavoidable.

Reducing the Carbon Footprint

As social responsibility gains focus in the workplace, many employees, especially those in the Millennial generation, are drawn to organizations with "green" initiatives. In fact, a key driver of engagement among Millennials is corporate social responsibility. Employers are therefore searching for ways to reduce their carbon footprint in order to draw this new generation of workers to their organizations and keep them engaged.

When people work virtually, especially from home, the number of cars sitting on the road, bumper to bumper, not moving during rush hour is greatly reduced. With this reduction comes a huge decrease in air pollution and fuel consumption from those immobile cars. Even now, the current population of virtual employees emits 51 million fewer tons of greenhouse gas.[14] Think of how much would be saved if the entire population of individuals who could work remotely did so full-time. With each reduction of gas emissions afforded through virtual work policies, organizations can increase their reputation as an organization that is "going green."

Some states are already offering incentives to encourage employees to work remotely so as to cut emissions resulting from commuting. Virginia, for example, offers companies up to $35,000 in tax breaks if they provide benefits such as laptops and other supplies for virtual employees. Maryland offers a $500 tax credit for any employees who establish a home office. Georgia offers $120 per employee if an organization implements a virtual work program.[15] Many other states are following suit in an attempt to improve the air quality and compliance with federal environmental standards.

Managers and employees can also cut emissions by a reduction in business travel; when employees work around the globe, they are local to clients and can conduct business without ever having to leave the area.

Increased Productivity

Contrary to what many managers think, research has shown that employees who work remotely are actually more productive than their counterparts in the office: 81 percent of remote American workers believe they are as productive or more productive in their home office compared to their business office.[16] Remote workers may actually accomplish *more* for the organization, contributing to a higher output and larger profit.

Think about the multitude of interruptions employees face on a daily basis in the office environment: coworkers stopping by to chat, long lunches, overhearing conversations in the hall. Have you ever been on a roll, completely immersed in a project, and all of a sudden a knock on your door completely throws off your concentration? After answering the door and speaking with the individual, you cannot quite remember your thought process. This is a very common scenario in the work environment, and each of these interruptions, no matter how brief or important, cuts a little time off an employee's productivity for the day. In fact, employees spend up to two hours a day not working, not including lunch and scheduled breaks.[17] Those two hours can often be attributed to interruptions. Although interruptions should be seen as ideal opportunities to establish dialogue and communication, they do take time from various other projects an employee must accomplish. Virtual work policies allow workers to establish their own time lines for when they can take breaks, thereby decreasing interruptions during their most productive times.

The reduction in time spent commuting contributes to increased productivity as well. The time previously used to get to and from work becomes discretionary time employees can use as they wish. Whether they complete more work, as is often the case,[18] or handle personal matters during this time, employers will benefit. Often, employees simply cannot stay late, even if they want to, due to personal obligations that begin at a certain hour. However, when working remotely, virtual workers often have more time to fulfill these obligations because they do not have to worry about the commute. Therefore, they can focus on projects they are completing later in the day, if they so desire. Time formerly spent commuting may also be replaced by exercise and getting more sleep, which contribute to fresh thinking and sharper minds. Remote workers will be ready and willing to contribute more at work when they are able to relax to a greater extent during their off-hours.

HEALTH AND WELLNESS

Taking Breaks

It is a very good argument that, physiologically, humans are not meant to sit in one place for eight or more hours per day. But because this practice is seen as the best way to get work completed efficiently, it has turned into not only a workplace standard, but also an expectation of many employers. Although employees may be free to take breaks throughout the workday to have lunch, go to the restroom, or stretch their legs, many people think taking frequent breaks can give colleagues the impression that they aren't getting much work done. For this reason, employees often end up sitting for hours in the same position without taking a break.

It is important to take a step back and think about the effects this can have on a person's health and well-being. You've experienced it: Your shoulders start to feel sore and achy. You know you have a tendency to slouch and you often correct your posture, but soon find yourself hunched over your keyboard again. Your butt starts to go numb from sitting in one place for so long, and your eyes feel strained from concentrating on your computer screen. Your body is telling you to get up and walk around, stretch, or simply get some fresh air. You want to listen, but you know you would get strange looks from your coworkers and your boss if you started doing calisthenics in the aisle or walking laps around the building. So you continue to sit in your chair. You might get up and take a trip to the water cooler, but that one minute of walking doesn't make you feel better for long.

In addition to the physical toll of office life, sometimes you just need a mental break from your assignments. After concentrating on a project for a long time, you feel as though you are no longer being productive. In times like these, it is best to take a break to mentally recoup and decompress. According to research presented by the American Psychological Association and Stanford University, people are actually more successful when they take breaks at their own discretion. Through studying a group of musicians, researchers determined that the success of individuals was more closely tied to time management and the approach to practicing than natural talent. Students who practiced in short bursts of intense con¬centration and took frequent breaks ultimately became better musicians than those who practiced nonstop, even if the frequent breaks led to less time practicing overall.[19] Researches concluded that the reason students who took more breaks were more successful was because they allowed themselves time to mentally recover, avoiding burnout and exhaustion.

These findings easily translate to the workplace. However, when working on-site, taking frequent breaks can be difficult. Again, you don't want colleagues to think you aren't working, so surfing the Internet, making personal phone calls, and reading a magazine at your desk are probably not the best options. There aren't always a lot of other choices for taking a quick mental break, unless you go chat with coworkers and distract them from working on their own projects. So, you try to power through the rest of the workday without taking a break. For the most part, this includes staring blankly at your screen and heading home that evening feeling exhausted.

What I've just described is a reality for many employees who work at their organization on-site. These physical conditions and frustrations play a large role in what people actually *do* while they are working. Even if you like the type of work you are doing and find it interesting, you can likely still relate to the aforementioned feelings. This is because *how* you do your work is just as important as *what* you are working on.

Now let's think about what the work experience is like when you work from home. When your body starts getting tired from sitting in one place, you get up and stretch. Your laptop gives you the freedom to rotate among your desk, the kitchen table, and the couch, so you are always comfortable when you're working. When you need some fresh air, you step outside for a moment or simply open a window. If you start to feel isolated, you go to the coffee shop down the street for a change of scenery.

I can personally attest to the value of getting out and taking a break. When I started my first company near Washington, D.C., I worked down in the basement, which also served as my bedroom. On average, I was working 14-hour days. Not only was being alone that much for so long difficult, but I started to feel that the room was becoming confining. Had I not built a regular break into my day, I would have gone crazy. Thus, I made it a regular practice at lunchtime to go for a great 3-mile run, and then bring lunch out to the nearby neighborhood pool, swim 20 laps, and sit in the sun eating my lunch. Not only did this eradicate any sense of claustrophobia, but I also met and interacted with multiple people while at the pool, which erased my sense of isolation.

In essence, I was in control of my environment. Virtual workers across locations likewise have similar control and can utilize it to their advantage.

Do you think a person who is thinking about how tired he is of sitting and how much he wants to take a break will be as productive as a person who is thinking about her job duties? Certainly not. Therefore it is in employers' best interests to support an environment where employees are physically comfortable, and virtual work is often a great solution.

Working virtually thus decreases stress and makes individuals overall more comfortable and relaxed, and employees can often apply greater focus to their tasks as well. Additionally, when workers realize their managers and organizations are helping to diminish stress levels among team members, they are more likely to feel that the organization cares about them. Remote employees are thus more inclined to put forth effort in return, which contributes to higher productivity and better business outcomes.

Reducing Absenteeism

With the availability of flexible work options, employees can work around personal responsibilities or illnesses without taking a day off work, thereby reducing the number of absences and, by extension, the costs associated with absenteeism.

Team members sometimes stay home when they have a minor cold or illness, but the only factor truly holding them back from work is the daunting trek to get there. If given the opportunity to work from home, many employees would take this option rather than taking a sick day. Additionally, illness tends to spread through the office like wildfire. When individuals are in close proximity, it is easy for germs to spread. During times when the risk of flu is high, employees are warned to stay home if they feel there is any chance they are infected. However, many employees do not want to use their sick days or paid time off, so they disregard this message. Implementing a virtual work policy will decrease the likelihood of a widespread flu outbreak, as employees will likely be more willing to work remotely rather than "waste" a sick day.

Absenteeism as a result of inclement weather, natural disasters, or other unforeseen issues can also be reduced. Blizzards that close roads and schools, storms that knock out electricity in certain areas—these occurrences lead to the necessity of closing offices, not least of which because employees with young children are often forced to take a day off when elementary schools are closed due to bad weather and childcare is unavailable. But if employees have the option to work virtually, business would no longer be put on a standstill when bad weather hits; employees can simply work from home, and productivity doesn't suffer.

It has been shown that remote work policies reduce absenteeism by 3.7 days per year, on average.[20] Consider an organization with 200 employees who each take five days off per year due to illness. The absenteeism rate for this particular organization would thus be 1,000 days per year. If employees are permitted to work virtually, however, the number of sick days goes down to an average of 1.3 days per year, therefore reducing absenteeism rates at this organization to only 260 days per year. Now consider an organization with 4,000 employees, and the figure is staggering.

The reduction in absenteeism can save organizations thousands of dollars. The estimated per-employee cost due to absences is $789 per year.[21]

Thus, with 200 employees the aforementioned organization could lose more than $157,000 as a result of unscheduled absences. In fact, the nation's largest employers estimate unscheduled absences cost their organizations $760,000 a year, on average.[22] Decreased attendance contributes to a decline in productivity, both from the absent employee and from his coworkers. Confusion about who should cover which duties invariably leads to wasted time, poorer-quality outcomes, and, in some cases, even safety violations and/or hazards. Virtual managers will see the benefits of reduced absenteeism when allowing employees to work virtually.

The aforementioned benefits of virtual employees positively affect organizations in a multitude of ways:

- Virtual work policies can be leveraged to attract and retain top talent, contributing to a reputation of excellence and high-quality output.
- Organizations will save on unscheduled absences, and contribute to a healthier earth.
- Remote workers can reach diverse customer bases, contributing to a competitive advantage and greater profits.
- Virtual managers will see a reduction in overhead costs, and an increase in productivity.

At first blush, distance workforces seem to be an ideal option for employers. However, no good decision is ever made without considering both sides, so let's take a look at the challenges associated with virtual workers.

THE CHALLENGES OF HAVING A VIRTUAL STAFF

Communication

Communicating with a virtual staff is harder than with collocated employees for one very important reason: Communication through any vein other than face to face is simply not *natural*.

As human beings, face-to-face communication is the most instinctive way to communicate; in-person communication is an innate skill humans have been practicing for thousands of years. You *learn* to read and write, but you *begin* smiling and talking. Babies react to the combination of emotion, tone, and gesture associated with different patterns of speech from their very first day. Even before they learn to speak, babies can pick up on emotions. Between birth and one month old, children are attuned to the emotions around them. Around two to three months, babies begin to make sounds—their form of communication—and will accompany these sounds with a smile. They respond to communication cues, even without understanding the exact meanings of words.

Additionally, words alone do not always convey the intended message. Humans are most likely to understand messages when they have a combination of verbal and physical "hints." Hints include not only words said, but also the tone of voice, the look on one's face, and gestures. Take, for example, the phrase "excuse me." The words alone mean one thing, but think about how the tone of voice could change the meaning of that expression. Said politely, the tone could refer to someone passing you on the street or attempting to get your attention. Spoken sneeringly, "excuse me" could be sarcastic. The look on someone's face when saying those words further contributes to a better understanding of whether she is being sarcastic, facetious, or genuine.

Technology, such as phone or e-mail, limits the amount of external cues available. When working at a distance, hints offered through body language and facial expressions are not evident. Without these hints, added focus and brainpower are required to interpret communication. It takes more energy, motivation, and effort not only to interpret a point, but to make a point as well.

Along with the lack of physical hints come misunderstandings. Without external cues available to help individuals interpret information, miscommunications have a higher likelihood to occur. Deadlines may not be clear, points may be misinterpreted, e-mails may be misread, or phone calls may be misheard. Conflict could increase due to misinterpreted information or phrases received via technology, and disagreements and lack of accurate information might affect project outcomes and the overall effectiveness of virtual teams.

The bottom line is this: It's simply more work to communicate with virtual workforces.

Communication issues within the virtual workforce contribute to an ineffective remote team, and can cause managers to be hesitant to implement distance working. Managers need to establish effective practices and training for managing these communication challenges in order to handle any issues that arise. That way, the potential for disaster resulting from miscommunication is reduced.

Technology and Tools

Imagine working away on a report, and all of a sudden that little hourglass or spinning wheel appears on the screen. It's the circle/hourglass of death. The next thing you know, the screen goes black, and you feel the beginnings of dread in your stomach.

Now imagine taking an incredibly important phone call, only to have your cellular service drop the call seconds before the person on the other end provides critical information.

Still further, have you ever checked your e-mail repeatedly, wondering why you are not receiving a response to the important message you sent a few days ago? You finally decide to call the recipient, and upon speaking with him, you realize the e-mail somehow got lost in cyberspace. Now you've missed the deadline, and there is nothing to be done.

We've all likely experienced one or more of these scenarios. As handy as technology can be, there are definitely some drawbacks to it. Technology enables virtual workforces to succeed, but it does not always provide perfect channels of communication. Whenever people rely on a tool rather than an innate process, the chance of complications rises. In-person communication requires only one "tool": your body. Most people are well aware of how to use this "tool" in communicating with others. However, virtual employees' communication revolves around the use of a much greater amount of technology than their collocated counterparts, and so complications that could result from the use of tools are more detrimental.

Other technology issues virtual workers may face include dispersed data and speed. Regarding the former, if employees work on different computers when they are outside of the office, documents may be spread across several machines. Luckily there are programs such as GoToMyPC and other custom-built remote portals that allow you to access a computer from a different location, but it requires the program to be installed on both computers. Without those programs, forgetting files on various computers may put a roadblock in the progress of a project. Additionally, when employees remotely access a system from a distance, the speed is often slower. As such, less work may be accomplished.

Privacy is also a concern when communicating via tools. When interacting face to face, humans are often aware of who can hear their conversations or see what they are discussing. However, when a tool is thrown into the mix, channels can be crossed, information can be sent to the wrong person, and computers can be hacked. There is a greater possibility that the individual's privacy is limited.

Putting support at a distance may additionally hinder the successful virtual completion of a project; IT support is not necessarily as easily accessible for virtual workers. Sometimes people have to wait days before resolving technology issues due to the availability of parts or personnel. Delays due to technology problems could lead to inconvenience for coworkers, clients, and managers, especially if a project is on a tight deadline.

The bottom line is that tools of all kinds, though beneficial in many respects, have the possibility to greatly hinder virtual work. Effective virtual managers must be aware of possible challenges and proactively work to correct any issues.

Building Relationships

Remember the saying "out of sight, out of mind"?

Many people adhere to the philosophy that when you are not visible, you should not necessarily be considered. Most virtual employees will never interact face to face with many of their coworkers. This means they are less visible in the work environment, and the chance of coworkers "forgetting" about them may increase.

It is not as simple to establish a bond with a coworker when you work at a distance. Team members may not be as committed to establishing relationships with people they don't see on a daily basis, thus contributing to detachment among virtual workers. Leaders may get caught up in other aspects of remote workforces and forget to establish a cultural bond. Without this bond, employees will likely be less dedicated to the organization, thus contributing to disengagement.

Isolation among virtual employees adds to the chance of being forgotten. Because they are not necessarily interacting with all of their coworkers on a daily basis, personal bonds are not established as easily, conversations may be more focused on work rather than on personal matters, and the culture of friendship is not quickly advanced. Without the ability to interact face to face and have informal conversations (not via e-mail), employees may miss out on a vital opportunity to establish relationships and personal connections. After-work happy hours, lunch breaks, and other in-person events that contribute to feelings of friendliness and camaraderie among employees are not necessarily available to virtual employees, and so they may not only feel lost but also lack a loyalty to the organization, which may have been established through face-to-face and personal interactions.

Along these same lines, when employees work virtually, they are likely less inclined to feel as though they are part of an organization. The lack of strong friendships with coworkers, which are the "unsung hero of retention," will contribute to feelings of disconnect. Detached virtual employees may be uninvolved and less committed, and may even contribute a reduced amount of work, thereby hindering the organization's outcomes.

Managers need to consider ways to tie remote workers to the culture of the organization. In doing so, they can expect better business outcomes and a more effective virtual workforce.

Performance and Trust

A large concern often cited by management in their hesitance to accept a virtual work policy is lack of regulation and oversight given to employees who are not in the office. When employees are not working in the same vicinity as management, the ability to visually check in on them isn't there. Essentially, managers cannot see if employees are working when they say they are working.

Because of this, performance measurement is harder to establish. How does one measure whether an employee is working or not when she is across the world? When employees are visible at work, employers often assume they are working. Managers need to trust their employees to do the work assigned to them in a timely and effective manner.

The trust factor has a great impact on the effectiveness and acceptance of virtual work policies. It is *fundamental* to establish a culture of trust between management and remote employees.

Virtual workforces are the future. Remote employees have the potential to greatly impact your organization's bottom line, and will allow you to maintain a competitive advantage in the changing climate. To be most successful in implementing distance teams, you must carefully consider all of the aforementioned benefits, but don't overlook the challenges you are bound to face. The following chapters will provide you with incredibly effective tools and practices to truly make virtual teams work for you. I urge you to use these tools to their fullest potential; you won't regret it.

CHAPTER 2

BUILDING TRUST IN VIRTUAL TEAMS

The best way to find out if you can trust somebody is to trust them.

—Ernest Hemingway

One of the greatest challenges of managing virtual employees—if not *the* greatest—centers on the issue of trust. In a recent survey of senior leaders of large and Fortune 500 companies, nearly 60 percent of respondents said earning trust was a challenge for leaders of virtual teams.[1] The very fact that managers cannot see the people they manage raises trust issues. Not surprisingly, most of the primary qualitative and quantitative research on working virtually strongly suggests that the overwhelming majority of managers possess an inherent, almost natural belief that they cannot manage what they cannot see. Managers have been programmed to desire physically witnessing employees' presence and punctuality, and the number of hours worked. Much of the research goes well beyond that, even suggesting managers have a propensity to think employees who cannot be seen will engage in opportunistic, non-productive, and self-serving activities. The saying "When the cat's away..." is well-known because the mentality exists.

Think about it: The absence of physical contact eliminates the cues managers use to gauge acceptance and gain assurances, such as eye contact or body language. There are no informal, casual, water-cooler, or "Good morning, how was your weekend" conversations. There is no, "Hey, let's grab lunch today," or Friday night drinks so ubiquitous to the "normal" workplace. No fist-bumps or high-fives. These examples of spontaneity are noticeably absent in the desert of the remote work environment. Teams and team members are now physically and socially distanced from one another and forced to communicate via technology versus face-to-face social interaction. The phrase "out of sight, out of mind" speaks volumes as to the natural psychological insecurity created by working remotely. Here are some things managers think about their remote employees:

- "I wonder what time he got out of bed today and started working."
- "Is she really working the whole day, or just sporadically?"
- "Why isn't he answering the phone or responding to voice mail?"
- "I'll bet she is at the mall shopping."
- "Maybe he took the day off to extend the long weekend. He's probably up in the mountains skiing by now."

On the other side of the coin, you have virtual employees asking:

- "How come I have not heard from anyone today?"
- "I wonder if they have forgotten about me out here."
- "Where does my career go from here in my basement? I wish someone told me."
- "I was horrified when my dog Max started barking on that big client conference call. I hope I don't get into trouble."
- "I hope they think I am doing a good job."

In the face of all these questions, it is of the utmost importance for virtual leaders to establish trust among their employees. As Stephen R. Covey, author of *The 7 Habits of Highly Successful People*, points out, "Trust is the glue of life. It's the most essential ingredient in effective communication. It's the foundational principle that holds all relationships." Trust garners even more importance in the virtual team environment. For example, it takes four times longer to build trust in a virtual environment than it does in "the old normal" environment.[2] In addition, when country borders are crossed remotely, that resulting cultural diversity adds roughly 17 weeks to the time it takes a remote team to reach optimum cohesive effectiveness.[3] A virtual environment introduces greater complexities, roadblocks, and challenging nuances not witnessed in a more conventional work team.

That is not to say that virtual teams are condemned not to work or be effective. But for virtual teams to achieve peak success, they must be managed differently and with special care. Trust is the centerpiece of that care.

Trust cannot be mandated, of course; it must be earned. However, it is difficult to earn trust when most of our interaction occurs via e-mail, intranet, and voice mail. So how does one make this trust come about, develop, and sustain itself for a virtual team?

CULTIVATE A REMOTE CULTURE OF FREEDOM AND AUTONOMY

Terrific virtual managers don't beat around the bush when it comes to the trust issue; they tackle it boldly and directly by doing one simple thing: *They let go*. Extraordinary virtual managers know that in order to let go and fully trust their employees, they must be very scrutinizing and careful during the talent selection process. By hiring only people they innately trust from the get-go, managers are able to start out on the right foot with new hires and support their autonomy. If working virtually is only a privilege for tenured employees, managers should choose their most trustworthy employees to work from home.

Virtual managers who cannot let go and continue to micro-manage, annoyingly checking in or checking up on their remote employees, will damage trust at their organization, and they have no one to blame but themselves. They should turn the reflective mirror back on themselves and realize that they don't have a trust issue; they have a hiring and talent acquisition problem. Simply put, they hired the wrong people. If, ultimately, a virtual manager cannot hire the right people and then trust them, then maybe that manager is in the wrong position. This manager's manager needs to re-cast this person into a different role that does not have virtual direct reports.

A huge tangential benefit of letting go is that employees are then free to *develop themselves*. This was once wisely noted by the late Booker T. Washington, who said, "Few things can help an individual more than to place responsibility on him, and to let him know that you trust him."

Creating the freedom and autonomy for trust with your virtual workers is the first and foremost objective of the most skilled and talented virtual managers; they make these two cornerstones a part of the organization's DNA.

Trust must begin with, and be led by, the virtual manager. As Lao Tzu, the famous Chinese Taoist philosopher, once said, "He who does not trust enough, will not be trusted."

FOSTER GREAT COMMUNICATION

It is not an accident that much of this book is dedicated to the topic of communication with, and to, the virtual employee. In reading the best practices highlighted here, one cannot help but notice that the regularly emphasized building blocks imperative to great communication center on consistency and reliability. Relationships of trust must be built on a foundation of consistent and reliable communication.

ENCOURAGE TRUST AMONG *EVERYONE*

Management should recognize that simply trusting an employee is not enough. Teamwork requires trust from all sides, and the most successful virtual teams are no different. Management must foster a culture of trust between employees to create the most engaged and driven virtual workers.

Managers can utilize games, humor, and fun to yield greater trust in each other individually and within the team. There is strong statistical and qualitative evidence to suggest that fun fertilizes employee engagement. Games, joking, and story telling can help build camaraderie and trust among remote team members. You may even choose to create a virtual community as the delivery vehicle for such fun, humor, and games. Some organizations have even gone so far as to regularly promote online video games between remote team members, such as once a week for an hour on a Friday afternoon. Importantly, in order for these online communities and activities to work, everyone should be expected to participate. Whereas *mandated* connotes negative strong-arming, *expected* does not. Strong virtual managers will afford inclusion and expect all remote employees to actively participate. Ideally, the chosen games should:

1. Interest all team members.
2. Be selected in such a way that "winning" can only be possible if there is good collaboration and teamwork.
3. Encourage, inspire, and teach good communication.

The cold reality is that very few virtual teams will find mutual trust and ultimate success without some in-person, social, face-to-face interaction. This is especially true during the earliest stage of a virtual team's evolution when rapport and relationships are first being established, so smart virtual managers will spend the time, money, and effort to get remote workers physically together at the team's birth or nascent stage.

In addition, the most adept virtual managers will plan for periodic on-site team meetings or even regularly fly the virtual employee into work at the head office for a week. Naturally, an opportunity to implement a formal team-building exercise should be seized upon; these would be most effectively applied if done when all team members are physically together.

ELUCIDATE AND DIRECT STAKEHOLDER EXPECTATIONS

Fantastic virtual managers aptly recognize that virtual teams often possess multiple stakeholders, each of whom may have different preferences and expectations for and about the team. Taking the proactive step of understanding stakeholder expectations up front can quickly eradicate virtual headaches down the road, especially relating to misunderstandings resulting in loss of trust. For instance, ensuring that each stakeholder group feels that they were afforded an opportunity to express opinions on the team's clarity of purpose, governing rules and policies, and goals will soundly set the stage for a virtual team's success. Whether the stakeholder is "corporate," "senior management," the virtual manager, the remote employee, or even the end customers of the virtual team, garnering this stakeholder buy-in at the outset obviates the possible conflicts, roadblocks, process inhibitors, and virtual landmines that could occur during and throughout the virtual team's evolution.

HR Solutions' Research Institute conducted thousands of focus groups, which effectively identified the seven most meaningful questions to ask each stakeholder related to a virtual team; the most distinguished and successful virtual managers will ask these seven key questions to each stakeholder:

1. What do you feel is the purpose of the team?
2. What are its related mission, vision, and values?
3. What are the outcomes we are targeting for success and how will we measure them?
4. What are our time lines for achievement of these outcomes, both short-term and long-term?
5. What do you feel are the perceived or real obstacles standing in the way of our success?
6. What do you feel your roles and responsibilities are as it relates to the virtual team?
7. What are your preferences for how we celebrate our team's successes when we achieve them?

Interestingly, this type of probing assessment has the tangential benefits of unveiling what support, resources, and competencies will be needed to ensure the virtual team's proficiency.

When stakeholders, both within the organization and outside of it, clearly understand what each individual hopes to achieve through virtual teams, undermining, misunderstandings, and other negative outcomes will be reduced. In illuminating each stakeholder's motivations and end-goals, trust can be established, as individuals will be less worried about being cheated in the interest of another stakeholder "getting ahead."

ESTABLISH AND MAINTAIN CLEAR AND COMPLEMENTARY ROLES AND RESPONSIBILITIES

As a natural outgrowth of the seven questions just posed, and especially from question number six, successful virtual managers recognize the importance of balancing freedom and autonomy with the necessary roles and responsibilities of the organization. Remote managers must make clear to each employee the role he or she plays in the outcomes of the virtual team. When virtual employees understand exactly what they need to do and are invested in their roles, they will remain loyal and dedicated to the organization. Virtual management can embrace this loyalty and recognize it as a stepping stone indicative of trust.

If you don't know where you are going, you will wind up somewhere else.
—Yogi Berra

The very fact that the team members are apart, far-flung, and separated makes it even more imperative that direction and roles be plainly spelled out. Alluding to Jim Collins's awesome book, *Good to Great*, I ask: Where is the bus going, and in which seat is everyone sitting?

The clarification of roles and responsibilities should begin with the virtual manager's early assessment of each team member's skill set, experience, strengths, and weaknesses. In addition, clarifying roles and responsibilities allows the virtual manager to leverage the fifth most impactful driver of employee engagement: job content and the ability to "do what I do best." If at all possible, the virtual manager should simply design and tailor the roles and responsibilities toward the remote employee's job content preferences and related skill sets, thereby fostering more employee engagement within the team.

Furthermore, one outgrowth and benefit to clarifying roles is that unmistakably unambiguous roles will afford far better optimization and alignment of team resources to produce the best business results.

Maslow's Hierarchy of Needs

IDENTIFY, UNDERSTAND, AND AMPLIFY EACH TEAM MEMBER'S MOTIVATORS

Whereas money certainly helps achieve the basic human Maslow hierarchy need of putting food on the table and a roof over our heads (the safety sphere represented in the triangle on page 37), the most impactful stimulants are:

- Becoming emotionally engaged and passionate about our work.
- Setting clear goals.
- Establishing a laser-focus on those goals.
- Experiencing the thrill and reward of personal and team success.

Through extensive research, HR Solutions has found **10 Key Drivers of Engagement** common among most employees. Each of these drivers will be discussed in more detail in Chapter 5. For now, suffice it to say that these motivators can be leveraged to create virtual employees who are dedicated to the virtual team, are invested in its outcome, and, most importantly, can be fully and wholly trusted to work at a distance.

Act on the Discovery of Distrust and/or Poor Performers

All of the considerations I've discussed thus far are incredibly effective means of building the organizational architecture of trust within and around your virtual team, but there will be times when a remote worker or manager displays behaviors or actions that lead to mistrust or worry on your part. Should this occur, do not delay—take action immediately. You may have a termite eating at your architecture, and if so, that termite will reproduce, destroying all the trust-building you have previously done.

HIRE THE RIGHT VIRTUAL MANAGERS

The most extraordinary virtual teams begin with virtual leaders who are willing and able to trust and mentor virtual employees to achieve the best outcomes. The best virtual managers will establish a culture of success and trust across locations. Sage virtual senior leaders will make sure they are hiring other virtual managers who possess rock-solid skill sets as communicators and collaborators. Ultimately, these two characteristics are critical to successful management of the virtual worker. In fact, more than half (57 percent) of top business leaders who are interviewing for virtual manager positions report that they are seeking candidates who exhibit excellent communication and collaboration skills.[4]

The right virtual managers will be:

- Visible at all times.
- Proactive.
- Open and active listeners.
- Willing to provide feedback.
- Good at follow-through.
- Adaptable.
- Direct.

Being Visible at All Times

In the virtual realm, being simply "visible" in the technical sense of the term is not effective; you cannot just be there and think your presence in the office is enough to make a difference. Management must be *actively* present at all times by taking the initiative to return e-mails and phone calls. Great virtual managers will go above and beyond to reach out to their direct reports and guarantee these employees know they matter and the virtual manager does care about them, despite not always being physically visible.

Research shows there is a positive correlation between visibility and perceived care: When employees perceive that management is actively involved in the organization, they will believe they are cared for and that they matter. Managers who answer e-mails on time, return phone calls, and make an effort to remind employees that they are there to help will likely be perceived as more visible. This way, employees will feel they matter to the organization, and will put forth extra effort for the best business outcomes.

Being Proactive

Virtual managers must go out of their way to take the initiative and question their virtual employees about what is being done, what needs to be done, and how these employees are handling working at a distance. The best candidates for virtual leadership are those who are willing to take the initiative to make the virtual team the best it can be. These candidates are individuals who think outside the box to accomplish better outcomes for working virtually. They will proactively communicate with their virtual reports, and take the initiative to establish a connection with these individuals regardless of the distance.

Being Open and Active Listeners

Virtual managers must be active listeners. They need to be keenly aware of what virtual employees are saying and what they desire, in order to bridge the separation. Effective virtual managers must be even more willing to listen to their employees' suggestions. I believe that a virtual employee who has a lot of thoughts may be even less inclined to act on them because she doesn't see coworkers or managers. Virtual managers must be willing to ask employees what they would like or what ideas they have, and should do their best to implement these ideas. It's better to know than not to, especially when it comes to new ideas and thoughts. Allow employees to contribute by hearing them out. Use their ideas. Change a "what if?" mindset to a "why not" mindset. Take a few risks along the way. You never know what will happen.

Being Willing to Provide Feedback

The art of giving feedback is *huge* in the virtual realm. Virtual employees want to know how they are doing, and fantastic candidates for virtual leadership positions will meet this desire.

Feedback is a complicated concept in the work environment. It often seems more negative or like criticism when coming from a personally removed individual (such as a boss) rather than a close relative or friend, and it is more acceptable for individuals with whom you have a close relationship to provide comments or considerations. For example, would a stranger or a close friend be more likely to mention that your zipper is down or that you have spinach in your teeth? Additionally, in which scenario would you be most embarrassed? I won't speak for everyone, but I would probably blush deepest if a stranger pointed either of those things out. On the other side of the coin, imagine *you* observe someone with his fly down. My guess is you would be more likely to point this out if he is a close friend. In the work world, the manager is not a close friend or family member. Without a close relationship, feedback will likely be viewed as negative, thereby embarrassing workers or causing them to feel like a disappointment. This is especially true in the virtual environment, as virtual employees may not have as close a relationship with their virtual managers as on-site employees do. The possibility of negative interpretations, combined with many people's hesitance to highlight other's mistakes, makes feedback a hard subject in the working world.

The irony is that management-provided feedback is the *ultimate* feedback, indicating that the manager cares. It shows she is taking the time to help, and employees should recognize this assistance. In becoming cognizant of what feedback really means, virtual employees can recognize the benefits, both in terms of productivity and in remaining connected to the organization. Through feedback, remote workers can see themselves through the manager's eyes. Leadership's comments can show that the manager is excited about the employee having a long-term career with the organization, and point out areas in which the employee shines. Additionally, feedback gives employees the opportunity to strengthen their skills.

The best virtual manager candidates are those who feel comfortable providing feedback, despite the commonly accepted "norms" previously discussed. Additionally, they must understand the impact feedback will likely have on employees, and be open and willing to alter the way they provide feedback to their virtual employees. In doing so, everyone will benefit from constructive criticism as well as positive comments.

Being Good at Follow-Through

Virtual managers are guaranteed to succeed if they always follow through with what they say. Even if a project or promise cannot be achieved, great remote managers will explain to employees exactly what happened. Virtual employees are working at a distance and may therefore feel isolated, but by following through with every promise and ensuring that every e-mail is answered, virtual employees will be more likely to feel that they truly are a part of the organization and that they really do matter. As a result, organizational outcomes will personally matter to the employee, thus keeping him engaged and willing to exert effort for the most business success.

Being Adaptable

Just as virtual managers do, virtual employees will face challenges. Understanding exactly how virtual work affects virtual teams will allow virtual managers to successfully alter practices for the most success. Virtual managers must be flexible and adaptable, taking changes in stride. Remote work policies often begin as experiments of some sort, and effective virtual managers must be able to incorporate any findings from these experiments into policies, thus creating the best virtual team. A very strong argument can be made to only hire managers who have had the experience of working virtually themselves.

Being Direct

Poor virtual managers have a bad habit of conflict avoidance and tend to tolerate non-performance. Thus, when hiring for virtual managers, make sure you use hiring parameters and behavioral interview questions that measure and assess the existence of conflict management, a key management trait. Directness is incredibly important in the virtual realm, as communication is often limited to e-mail and phone calls, which often require short, succinct messages. Beating around the bush is detrimental to effective communication and understanding across the distance. Virtual employees will benefit most from open, direct information, and from virtual managers who are not afraid to get straight to the point.

The absolute best leaders will encompass these traits and utilize each to their utmost advantage. Leadership is key; organizations must hire strong and extraordinary virtual leaders who are willing to put forth effort to engage employees across the separation. In doing so, teams will never fail to achieve the best virtual outcomes.

Case Study: Cisco

Creating the most effective virtual teams starts with employing the best leaders. With their motto, "Together, we are the human network," at the forefront of the organization, Cisco Systems, a global technology and networking firm, is intent on shaping the future of the Internet and creating a connection across individuals, groups, and locations. Senior leadership is determined to change the way humans interact. Through their dedication to innovation, their close relationship with technology, and a customer base that transcends global boundaries, the organization has developed a necessity for virtual work. "Global workforce collaboration is a huge part of our DNA," says Mark Hamberlin, Worldwide Leader, Global Staffing.[5] Combining a formal virtual policy with part-time remote work, the organization allows many of its more than 71,000 employees to work at a distance. In doing so, Cisco really can create a true global network.

Through virtual work and technology, Cisco has been able to cast a wider recruitment net for top talent, whether they are hiring line-level employees, virtual workers, or management. Although leadership does not necessarily screen candidates for remote work, the *possibility* of virtual work offered through the organization allows them to recruit the candidates most suitable for the culture and responsibilities required for each position. When the right foundation is in place, people can be successful anywhere.

Employing great virtual managers is imperative to creating thriving virtual teams, and so virtual leaders at Cisco are hired based on their ability to "C-LEAD":

Collaborate

Learn

Execute

Accelerate

Disrupt

During interviews for virtual management positions, leaders at Cisco ask behavioral questions to get a better view of how well candidates embody these traits. "For example, with regard to [collaboration], we will ask applicants who might work remotely how they gain trust, build relationships, and work across boundaries," states Hamberlin, "We want to know how well they are able to build a network." Additionally, Cisco looks for other qualities that define a successful virtual leader: being naturally proactive, having good communication skills, and having a degree of comfort with ambiguity. Searching for a candidate with this combination of qualities increases the likelihood of hiring extraordinary virtual managers.

At Cisco, effective remote management is so important that it is ingrained in management new hires from day one, when managers are taught to use the most applicable technologies for the virtual world, such as video conferencing. Additionally, managers must undergo rigorous training courses where interacting with and managing remote teams is specifically highlighted. Visibility is fundamental in the Cisco virtual world, and effective virtual managers are encouraged to establish a relationship with employees despite the physical gap. In creating this relationship and maintaining visibility of virtual managers, employees at Cisco remain engaged no matter where they are located. Because engagement fosters effectiveness both on-site and in the virtual world, virtual managers can expect success when they create a relationship that will keep their virtual employees dedicated and loyal.

To productively lead virtual teams, virtual managers must also be engaged in the culture of the organization, as culture fit is a huge indicator of success for employees and managers alike at Cisco. "The challenge is how to instill Cisco culture in remote workers," says Hamberlin. "If someone cannot manage the culture and performance requirements, [he or she] will not survive in Cisco whether or not [he or she] work[s] remotely." Similar to other organizations with virtual workforces, Cisco struggles with the challenge of establishing a sense of culture in virtual employees when these employees do not physically experience it daily. It is often hard for new hires to become accustomed to the way an organization functions when they are not directly immersed in the culture. Effective virtual managers at Cisco are those individuals who go beyond the call of duty to establish a culture in which everyone feels connected. Additionally, virtual leaders incorporate the culture into their own attitudes and behaviors; when they have adopted the culture, it will be more likely to shine through in their interactions with their direct reports, increasing everyone's involvement in the culture as well.

To further maintain engagement, virtual managers at Cisco develop creative ways to recognize their employees in various locales. Instead of directly calling or speaking with an employee, management often provides recognition via e-mail. This e-mail can then be forwarded to whomever it concerns, so visibility of a job well done is widespread. Additionally, Cisco offers recognition for employees during virtual meetings by allowing employees and management to vote electronically on the spot for an employee they feel best embodies the requirements for various awards. This award is shared with the entire team, across all Cisco locations, so "you still get applause around the world," Hamberlin states. Creating a culture of recognition that bridges the gap between the physical and remote world will keep employees engaged despite the distance.

In hiring the right people to lead their virtual teams, and then giving these individuals the ability to utilize drivers of engagement to keep their virtual direct reports engaged, Cisco is changing the way people live and work and creating an inclusive human network, despite the physical separation. Success often begins with leaders who will guide others along the path to triumph.

Each of the traits described in this chapter boils down to engagement: Leaders who are dedicated, invested, and committed to an organization will be the most likely to fully embody each characteristic of extraordinary virtual leaders. Engaged leaders foster engagement in virtual workers who will be worthy and capable of being trusted. Because trust is the foundation of a virtual team, organizations will benefit from hiring virtual leaders. Thus, make sure you are both hiring and developing engaged remote managers. In turn, these leaders will exert effort to hire and develop the absolute best virtual employees.

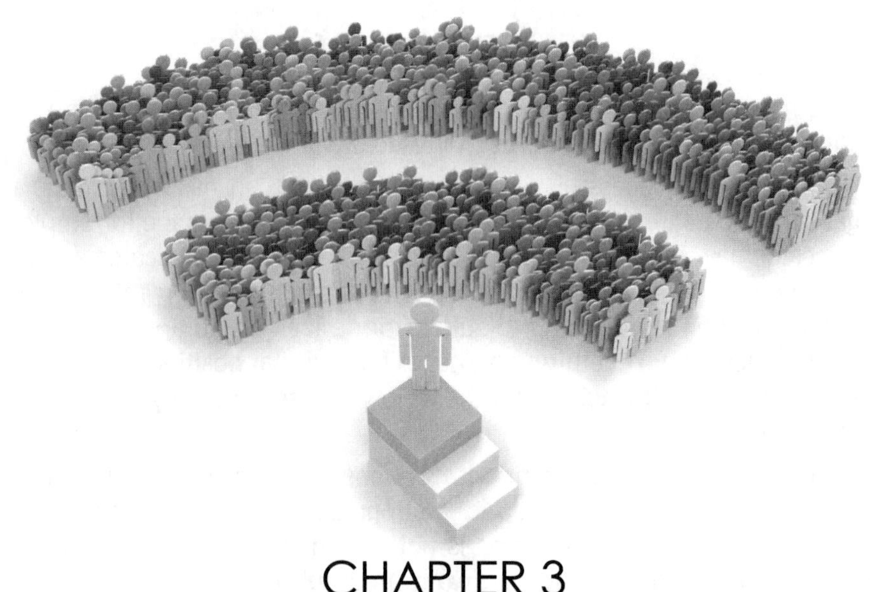

CHAPTER 3

QUALITIES OF TOP VIRTUAL EMPLOYEES

THE FOUR KEY "SELF" CHARACTERISTICS

According to a recent survey statistic, approximately 24 percent of employed persons in America did some or all of their work at home in 2010.[1] Not a surprising data point given the ease with which modern technology facilitates the logistics necessary for virtual work. With Skype, instant messaging, and Webinars just a click away, workforces worldwide are more in touch than ever.

What are surprising, however, are findings regarding the U.S. workforce's *desire* to work from home. Approximately 40 percent of employees claim that the opportunity for a virtual work arrangement is a deciding factor when selecting an employer,[2] and when asked to rank job attributes, a large percentage of employees apprized the opportunity to work from home above attractive benefits such as stock options and daycare.[3]

Furthermore, Millennials employees are known for expecting the work/life equilibrium and flexibility afforded by virtual work.[4]

Therefore, a successful virtual work program can easily earmark an organization as an employer of choice and be a key advantage for employers seeking new talent. I think it's fair to say, assuming pay scales and job descriptions are on par with industry standards, the hiring manager for a virtual position is not going to suffer from a lack of job applications. In fact, the question for the hiring manager for a virtual position is not "How do I solicit job applicants?" but rather "How do I select the right candidate for the job?"

I'll cut straight to the point with my answer: The right candidate for the job is not the job applicant with a strong *desire* to work from home. A strong desire for a virtual position is not a predictor of employee engagement. At the end of the day, you want an employee who wants the *job*, not the benefit of virtual work, and therefore I contend many of the best predictors for employee engagement in a virtual position are no different from the predictors of employee engagement in a position on site. Passion, loyalty, professionalism, and applicable skills and knowledge are all essential characteristics when you expect an employee to contribute to and not detract from a magnetic culture.

But let's face it: Virtual employees are on an honor system, more or less. You, as the hiring manager, need to trust that you are hiring people who are working when they are supposed to be working, and because the employee-manager relationship in a virtual work arrangement requires more trust, virtual employees not only need to embody the essential characteristics of engaged employees, but they also need to demonstrate in abundance what I call the four "self" characteristics. Engaged virtual employees are:

- Self-starters.
- Self-motivated.
- Self-disciplined.
- Self-sufficient.

Let's take a look at each characteristic on its own.

Self-Starters

As the hiring manager for a remote position, you want a virtual employee to be a self-starter. When not on-site, the employee is essentially free from the regular, external prodding or stimulus on-site workers receive from managers or coworkers to stay on task. There is no boss standing in the next room, and no executive to pass by and observe whether the employee is responding to client requests in Outlook or posting updates on Facebook. You need to know your virtual employee can perform without these physical cues.

What Does a Self-Starter Look Like?

Self-starters display three common attributes. First, to a self-starter, the absence of external stimuli to stay on task makes no difference. These employees do not have to be reminded to work, nor do they call their boss and ask what to do next. On the contrary, self-starters *seek* work. Their assumption is that they are doing something at all times to earn their paycheck.

Example of a Self-Starter:

Anne is a Web developer for a small online media firm with headquarters in Europe. On Friday, Anne experiences a down period at work. Her European counterparts have the day off to celebrate a national holiday. Anne handed off a key site upgrade project to the development team on Thursday, and the specs for her next initiative will not be finalized until Monday. Anne chooses to read a whitepaper on industry trends, and finds the content compelling, so she puts together a brief summary of the paper's key points and distributes it to her peers.

Second, self-starters assume responsibility. Self-starters recognize it is their job to contribute to a magnetic culture, and therefore perform their work as if they are the face of the business at all times, regardless of whether they are interacting with a client or with a peer. Though a self-starter might be sitting at home and working in his pajamas, he always conducts himself as the consummate professional.

Example of a Self-Starter:

Brian is a software developer for a mid-sized marketing firm. One day, Brian received a phone call from a client: Apparently, the new reporting software application developed by Brian and built by his peers was not performing as expected. Brian tells the client he will have a solution for the problem in hand by the end of the day, and then schedules a conference call with all critical parties to develop a strategy to correct the issue. Brian leads the call, takes notes, and sends a follow-up e-mail to all participants outlining what needs to take place, who is responsible for each task, and all associated deadlines. Brian calls the client to alert the client to the plan of action and communicate time frames.

Be forewarned: This willingness to assume responsibility can mean that self-starters have no problem adopting power to communicate and address key issues within the organization. Although this quality may seem off-putting to some managers, remember: Virtual employees are at an inherent disadvantage when it comes to solving problems. They lack the ability, for example, to run down to the IT department to expedite a client request and are often held hostage by e-mail inboxes and voice mail. Successful virtual employees will often think outside of the e-mail inbox and voice-mail system to connect to the right people, implement the appropriate strategy, and achieve the desired outcome. Self-starters may not always follow protocol, but in my experience, engaged virtual employees' techniques for working around classic corporate bottlenecks are often best practices for all.

Finally, self-starters finish. Self-starters know their role is not over until the job is complete, and these individuals define success as not just "giving a task their best shot," but also as seeing the task through to the end. It is this ability to strive for the finish line, big or small, that often makes self-starters excellent time managers as well. For example, a self-starter will create an agenda of no more than 30 minutes worth of content if they only have 30 minutes for a call, and they will derive satisfaction from covering each agenda item in full.

Example of a Self-Starter:

Carrie is a graphic designer, and was asked to create all of the images for a multi-page Website, hundreds in total. Carrie was told by her boss there was no immediate deadline and the Website was not her top priority. Carrie allocates a half hour at the end of every day to image design, and several days later completes the assignment.

Self-Motivated

For virtual employees to be engaged and successful, they need to be self-motivated. When not on site, the virtual employee is subjected to a variety of non–work related distractions: a chatty neighbor, a pile of dishes, or a favorite movie on television. Furthermore, there are occasionally down periods in a work day, and the temptation to make a quick trip to the grocery store or tackle that attic can be enticing. You, as the hiring manager, need to know that your virtual employees are motivated to work without requiring a carrot from you and regardless of distractions and temptations.

What Does Self-Motivation Look Like?

Self-motivated employees demonstrate two key competencies. First, self-motivated virtual employees are able to easily ignore the distractions of their remote office and zero in on the tasks at hand. How do they accomplish this laser-like focus? Self-motivated individuals are often single-minded, and the mantra goes something like this: "Achieve a goal without outside help." In my experience, the goal that motivates these employees varies from one individual to the next. For a recent graduate, the goal might be to pay off a student loan. For the account manager, the goal might be a satisfied book of business. For the marketing executive, the goal might be an ad campaign with a high return on investment. Regardless of the specific goal these individuals set, self-motivated employees have an extraordinary sense of purpose.

Example of Self-Motivation:

Molly is an entry-level marketing assistant at a boutique advertising agency. She enjoys her work, and her first performance reviews garner high marks. During Molly's most recent review, Molly tells her manager she is very interested in emerging social media trends and would like to work in this particular field. Molly's manager applauds this interest and informs Molly that within the next 12 months, the agency is going to create a social media group within the marketing department. Molly wants a position in this new group, and therefore identifies and attends every local seminar and Webinar on social media available. She updates her manager on her attendance and circulates key learnings among the department staff. Unasked, she outlines a social media strategy for one of the agency's clients and presents it to her manager.

Be forewarned: The extraordinary sense of purpose in self-motivated employees often leads them to take risks. They do not confine their behavior to their comfort zone, but instead try new ideas and test-drive new strategies to accomplish their goal. This too can be off-putting to a hiring manager, but remember: Wisdom is the byproduct of experience, and wisdom is a valuable asset in any organization. Wise employees easily adapt to change or to unfamiliar situations because they have a broad set of experiences from which to draw an action plan—crucial skills in a magnetic culture.

Finally, and in concert with the last point, self-motivated employees are lifelong learners. They are not afraid to admit to deficits in their knowledge and are willing to try new things to broaden their skill set. This particular characteristic is essential in a remote work arrangement, because virtual employees are again at an inherent disadvantage. They lack the intellectual stimulation readily available in work-related conversations with a coworker in the next cubicle or impromptu brainstorming sessions over lunch with the team. Even more notable: They lack visual cues from others that may indicate their communication is confusing or their reasoning is off. Therefore, it is critical for virtual employees to be in a constant state of self-evaluation, and be willing to take the initiative to actively pursue opportunities to learn and do more when they find their knowledge or skill set coming up short.

Example of Self-Motivation:

Nate is a Web developer for a large technology firm. To accommodate his wife's career, Nate has relocated to Hong Kong, and, for the first time, is working remotely. In the course of corresponding more frequently via e-mail, Nate realizes his written communication skills are not very strong. Nate researches online to gather business writing tips and requests permission from his manager to attend a Webinar on effective communication.

Self-Disciplined

This third "self" characteristic is typically what managers think of first when they think about desirable qualities in virtual employees. The term *self-disciplined* implies organization, time management, and responsibility. It suggests you as the manager will be free from watching over virtual shoulders and breathing down virtual necks.

These ideas are certainly not off base. Self-disciplined employees are not procrastinators and their work style is never disordered. I, however, like to think of self-discipline as a protein boost. When combined with the other "self" characteristics, it makes the whole virtual employee that much stronger. Think of it in terms of a heart surgeon: If you were undergoing a bypass, would you want an unmotivated but disciplined physician operating? Would you want a motivated but undisciplined physician operating? No, you want a motivated, disciplined surgeon performing the procedure.

What Does Self-Discipline Look Like?

Self-disciplined employees are easily recognized by three character traits: long-term focus, stellar time management, and a strong sense of organization. First, a self-disciplined employee is able to forego immediate pleasure and instant gratification in favor of attaining a more meaningful outcome. Self-discipline is particularly critical in a remote work setting, where the temptation to procrastinate is greater because the employee has more non–work related activities at her disposal.

Example of Self-Discipline:

Gwen is an accountant for a large bank. Gwen's boss gives her an assignment that must be completed by tomorrow morning. Gwen has plans to join her coworkers for lunch. She recognizes the tendency of her coworkers is to chat for an extended period of time. If she wants to complete the assignment, she knows she should eat lunch quickly and return to work, and yet she is looking forward to the camaraderie. Gwen ultimately decides to forego lunch with her coworkers to make sure she will have the project finished on time.

Be forewarned: Self-discipline can be a somewhat exotic skill. The Internet bubble promoted a trend wherein many employees were quickly gratified regardless of traditional performance cues such as education, experience, and execution. Although these employees in no way represented the majority of the U.S. workforce, the Internet bubble had a glamorous cache that appealed to our celebrity-obsessed culture, and there are plenty today who still chase the idea of big gains in a short time frame with minimal effort.

Second, in my experience, self-disciplined employees are masters of time management. They spend time on those activities that bring them closer to accomplishing their goals, and their work days are highly structured.

Example of Self-Discipline:

Chris is in sales and has worked from a virtual office for several years. Many of his prospects have international headquarters, and therefore Chris has to make sure he is contacting the decision-makers at appropriate times during the day. As a result, his schedule rarely varies. Mornings are for responding to e-mails; Fridays are for completing and submitting expense reports. At the end of every day, he updates his pipeline in Salesforce before retiring for the evening. He religiously uses the calendar function in Outlook to keep his routine running smoothly.

Last, self-disciplined employees not only apply structure to their time, but to their work space as well. For the remote virtual employee, organizing a space conducive to working is more difficult than an on-site employee, for whom desks, files, phone systems, and storage space are provided. Successful virtual employees create work spaces for themselves that mirror traditional office arrangements. I've heard this referred to as "BYOT" (or "Bring your Own Tools").

Example of Self-Discipline:

Sharon is a medical writer who works from home. Her children are of preschool age, so Sharon converted the room above the garage into her office to afford her the quiet she needs to write. The space is well laid out and complete with the necessary connections: phone, fax, and internet. Her computer software is updated, and she is careful to have a back-up system in place at home so that if for some reason she is ever without a connection to the shared office drive, she can still be productive. In addition, Sharon made the effort to make sure her desk and chair are ergonomically sound, so that she is not distracted by uncomfortable physical cues. Sharon makes sure the home phone line forwards directly to voice mail while she is working.

Self-Sufficient

Finally, the successful virtual employee is highly self-sufficient. These individuals are engaged employees despite having very little social interaction with peers and managers. This does not mean that for a virtual employee to be engaged, he must have an introverted tendency. On the contrary, successful remote sales personnel, for example, are characteristically highly extroverted individuals. It simply means that, introverted or extroverted, self-sufficient employees do not rely on a collegial atmosphere to get energy or foster creativity. They can do this on their own. They typically need little assistance and do not rely on coworkers for a boost of morale.

What Does Self-Sufficiency Look Like?

I know that an employee has the potential to be self-sufficient in a remote work setting when she displays three critical work habits. First, self-sufficient employees are typically highly effective communicators, and make no mistake, this is the most important skill set necessary for a remote employee to be successful. In fact, in a recent survey of virtual managers, 61 percent of those surveyed identified solid communication skills as the most desirable trait in a virtual employee.[5]

Self-sufficient virtual employees are able to efficiently and effectively deliver their message in a phone call, an e-mail, or via a teleconference. They do not need to sound their ideas out loud with a manager, toss a question over the cubicle wall, or pop into a colleague's office to facilitate a conversation. They return calls and e-mails quickly.

Example of Self-Sufficiency:

Carlos is an account manager and has been working from home for several years. Carlos understands he is at a disadvantage when communicating with his colleagues and clients from a remote location, and therefore he adopts certain tenets when corresponding and conversing remotely. First, Carlos pays attention to what others say, and makes sure his responses are concise, yet thorough. Second, Carlos also knows, for example, that the best way to up-sell a client is via a live conversation, and the best way to communicate with the operations team at the office is via e-mail. He therefore thinks about the appropriate communication channel (phone, instant message, e-mail) for his message and uses these vehicles to his advantage. Finally, he also knows how easy it is to be misunderstood without physical cues, and is therefore careful to maintain a neutral tone in his communication, proofreading his e-mails carefully to make sure nothing sounds condescending or patronizing.

Second, a successful virtual employee is emotionally self-sufficient as well. Because the majority of the communication with virtual employees takes place via phone and e-mail, virtual employees are essentially cut off from many nonverbal feedback cues. Therefore, the feedback they receive is of a lower quality than that of their on-site counterparts. Fortunately, emotionally self-sufficient employees have little need for guidance or input, and do not rely on peers or managers for performance feedback. On the contrary, they are self-confident and remarkably adept at assessing their own performance.

Example of Self-Sufficiency:

Jeff is in an entry-level business development position and works remotely. He is tied to a commission plan and measures his performance against his quota. Jeff works diligently to fill the pipeline for the national account executives and spends the majority of his time on the phone placing cold calls. Jeff derives immense satisfaction from a call that results in a valid lead, and through perseverance, has refined his skills over time.

Finally, self-sufficient employees have a high sense of organizational mission, despite working in a socially isolated environment. They believe their job responsibilities contribute to a larger whole and a greater good. This sense of mission guides their everyday activities and can be seen in their decision-making skills. When these employees are asked "What is your job?" they just might respond with "Customer satisfaction."

Example of Self-Sufficiency:

Janet is a customer service representative. She logs all of her calls and categorizes them in a weekly call report that she turns in to her manager. At the end of one particular week, Janet notices that she has handled a large volume of calls related to a print function issue. Janet brings the issue to her manager's attention, and then suggests that while the organization is resolving the issue, the customer service department send gift cards in a small denomination for an online print service to those customers affected by the problem.

SELECTING CANDIDATES FOR ENGAGEMENT

You owe it to yourself to find the best candidates available. This means you have to take your time and have a rigorous process in place for candidate sourcing, recruiting, and hiring.

The Job Description

One of the biggest challenges managers face when managing virtual employees is poor performance. Yes, poor performance can be the result of hiring the wrong individual into the position, but poor performance can also result from ill-defined job expectations. Therefore, it is imperative to establish expectations for a virtual position at the onset of the hiring process, and this begins with the job description.

Your goal when writing a job description for a virtual position is to be as specific as possible. Clarity will set expectations at the onset and reduce the number of unqualified applicants. Furthermore, when a description carefully outlines responsibilities and defines desirable attributes, it can be used as the basis for performance evaluations once the candidate is on board. The job description for your virtual position should clearly state the following:

- Description of the overall functions of the job.
- A clear, concise outline of the position's job responsibilities and tasks.

- The basic qualifications for consideration, including exact technical skills, soft skills, areas of expertise, credentials, and certifications.
- The attributes that underlie outstanding performance.
- Reporting relationships.
- Hours.
- Travel.
- Requisite equipment.

Note: As the business world migrates to a virtual model, it is increasingly important for organizations to hire employees with specific technological skills that make virtual teams successful. Therefore, I highly recommend that, for virtual positions, the "Basic Qualifications" section of the job description include a high aptitude for and experience with modern technology, particularly in collaboration/communication channels, such as Skype, Wikis, Web conferencing, virtual project management resources, and mobile messaging. Technology is the glue that solidifies your virtual workforce.

In addition, I strongly advise against simply creating a list of duties when writing a job description, particularly for a virtual position. Rather, your description should convey a sense of the role's identity within the organization and a specific list of *priorities*. Remember: Successful virtual employees are highly self-sufficient, which means they have a strong sense of mission. Explaining how the role fits into your corporate structure and stating a role's priorities in the job description appeal to this high sense of mission and serve as nice punctuation to the duties and tasks you define.

In my organization, a role's identity and specific priorities are included in the first two sections of the job description: "Overview" and "Primary Objectives." For example, if I were hiring for a virtual recruiter, those sections of my job description would resemble the following.

> Human Resources Recruiter
>
> **Overview:** The Human Resources Recruiter is responsible for recruiting success throughout the organization. This will be accomplished by developing and executing recruiting plans and working existing recruiting and sourcing strategies, as well as creating new ones. The Human Resources Recruiter will be a key driver in

the organization's success by attracting and hiring the best talent available.

Primary Objectives:

1. Create and execute sourcing and recruiting strategies.
2. Network through trade associations, industry contacts, thought leaders, employees, and business memberships.
3. Develop, coordinate, and execute recruiting at the college and university level.
4. Complete administrative and bookkeeping duties in a timely, accurate fashion.

Once you have a job description in place, the question becomes: Where is the best place to post for virtual positions? The answer is easy: post virtually! With modern technology, attracting the right employees is easier, quicker, and cheaper than ever, and if you're looking for someone who can stay connected to your organization virtually, then it stands to reason you should ask them to connect virtually in the first place.

I highly recommend posting on niche sites and forums. You'll automatically thin your pool and attract individuals specifically looking for work in your particular industry. For example, if I were an online media firm in Chicago, I would post my position on the Chicago Interactive Marketing Association (CIMA) Website. If I were searching for an accountant in Cleveland, I'd post on the Ohio Society of CPAs (OSCPA) Website. A quick search on Google will uncover dozens of possibilities, and in many instances, the posting process is easy and free.

Business networks such as LinkedIn are also an ideal way to identify and connect to virtual applicants, particularly when you are searching for a particular skill set or industry background, and it is easy to send a job description to your LinkedIn connections to generate virtual search momentum. Also, don't discount Craigslist. It is not as crowded as other job sites such as Monster and Indeed, and, for a small fee, you can post a position in a specific region and/or industry and leave the posting up for as long as 30 days. Even better: You can do a free search on resumes already posted in the "Services Offered" section. You never know what you might find, and reading through a seemingly qualified applicant's online post can give you an immediate sense of how he communicates in a virtual setting.

The Interview

In my experience, there is no better way to understand whether a job candidate's skill set matches your profile of an engaged, virtual worker than in a comprehensive, face-to-face interview. But whom to interview? I have three tests.

Test one: the resume screen. Normally, I would say solid skills and healthy doses of passion indicate a proclivity for engagement and thus outweigh actual work experience every time. You, the employer, can provide experience, and if the candidate is bringing the right personality and aptitude to the table, she will make the most of that experience.

This stance alters, however, for virtual positions. I do feel that when selecting candidates for a remote work arrangement, you are well advised to take a hard look at candidates who have demonstrated success working remotely in previous positions, and condense your applicant pool accordingly. The most obvious reason behind this strategy is pure logistics. Candidates who have already performed virtual work are more likely to have a remote office setting that accommodates telecommuting: phone lines, Internet connections, quiet space, and adequate storage, for example. They are well versed on how to organize their physical surroundings to minimize interferences and encourage productivity.

In addition, I believe that candidates who have previously held a virtual position and are seeking another remote work arrangement know what to expect. They are prepared for some of the pitfalls of virtual work: social isolation, an increased number of non–work related distractions, and limited feedback, to name a few. They have demonstrated their ability to engage with their employer despite these pitfalls, and enjoyed the opportunity enough to seek another remote position.

Once you have pre-screened resumes, test two is a phone screen. I cannot stress enough how critical this step is! One of your virtual employees' main communication channels will be the telephone, and it is important for you to assess their phone skills firsthand. Aside from the fact that phone interviews are relatively inexpensive and time efficient, I think one of the nice things about a phone interview is that you do not have to prepare a list of hardball questions and determine what appropriate answers will be in advance. Softball questions are just fine, and your job during the call is simply to listen to what is being said and how it is being said by the candidate. Pay attention to the following cues:

- Are responses to your questions quick and precise?
- Are the candidate's responses well organized and clearly articulated?
- Does the candidate enunciate?
- Does the candidate sound energized? Earnest?
- Does the candidate sound muffled or unprofessional?
- Does the candidate interrupt you?

Test three for me is an e-mail conversation. Assuming a candidate interviewed well over the phone, I like to initiate a little E-mail dialogue. My reasoning for this step is the same as my reasoning for step two: e-mail is a critical communication channel for all remote employees, and therefore I want to make sure the candidate expresses himself well in written form. I'll choose one follow-up question based on the phone interview, a question that warrants more than a yes-or-no response, and send it the candidate's way. I then look for the following cues in the response:

- Did the candidate respond in a timely manner?
- Does the response get right to the point?
- Is the response polite?
- Is the response specific?
- Does the response avoid what I refer to as "net slang," such as: "plz," or "u r," or "thx"?
- Is the response free from glaring grammar errors and misspellings?
- Does the response convey a professional image through word selection?

Finally, if a candidate has passed through my resume, phone, and e-mail filters, then it's time to meet him, and I will schedule a face-to-face interview. I know the biggest chances I have to impact the success of my organization are my hiring decisions, and therefore I need to create an additional opportunity to gauge applicants' potential and sell my organization. Also, traits such as presence, temper, and interest level are evidenced in facial gestures, in tone of voice, in speed of speech, and in movements, and when I evaluate an applicant, I want visual cues to corroborate or refute what I am seeing on paper and hearing out loud.

It is during this interview that I will throw the hardball questions in order to get a feel for the candidate's potential to be an engaged employee in my organization, and to determine whether she is an ideal fit for a virtual position. Ignoring important personality and work style preferences of candidates jeopardizes the success of any virtual workforce, and it is also essential to the on-boarding process to know any candidate's strengths and weaknesses on crucial virtual work skills and attributes. Therefore, I specifically ask questions to define to what extent the candidate exhibits the four "self" characteristics. I believe in structured interviews that focus on behavioral attributes to help me gather details. An intelligent and charismatic interviewee can project "all the right stuff," whether or not he has it, so I look hard for real examples and ask the applicant for as many as possible.

I cannot stress enough how important the trust factor is when hiring an individual into a virtual position. To assess trustworthiness, I always ask candidates to identify their biggest mistake in the last six months. This question often catches people off guard, but in my experience, when a candidate is forthright with her answer, she is demonstrating integrity and communicating to me that she is trustworthy. Sadly, most interview candidates do not pass this basic behavioral test. Most people either say they cannot think of a time when they made a mistake, or they bring up a situation in which a problem occurred, and put the blame on someone else. A lot of people want me to think they are perfect employees, which is not possible, because we are all human.

Two years ago, I was interviewing candidates for the open position of Senior director of projects at HR Solutions, and asked this question to all of the interviewees. I conducted nine interviews in which no one was willing to admit a mistake. I was starting to get a little discouraged. Finally, on the 10th interview, I spoke with someone who was open, forthcoming, and honest. I was meeting with a woman named Meredith Boza. When I asked her what her biggest mistake was, she quickly responded with "Well, that will be easy; we really messed this one up." She talked openly about what went wrong in her last position, what measures she and her colleagues put in place to ensure it wouldn't happen again, and what she had personally learned from the situation. I immediately trusted her and hired her on the spot, and she has been a vital part of our organization ever since.

In addition to the "Mistake Question," which I also fondly refer to as the "Deer in Headlights" question, I have found the following questions to be particularly powerful.

- Do you regard yourself as a self-starter? Can you give me a recent example of when you displayed this quality?
- Tell me about a time your manager was absent and you had to make a decision.
- If you had a problem and did not know the answer, how would you find the solution?
- Tell me about an occasion when you chose not to finish a given task.
- Describe a project in which you felt highly invested. How long did that feeling last?
- If you had enough money to retire right now, would you?
- Tell me about a goal you achieved which at some point(s) seemed hopeless. Why did you continue to persevere?
- Give me an example of a time when you set a goal, but you could not achieve it.
- Tell me at least three things you have done in the past 12 months to improve yourself, both business-wise and competency-wise.
- What are some areas in which you could improve? How will you improve?
- How do you stay current?
- How long do you expect to stay with us?
- How do you prioritize your projects?
- What are your work habit strengths and weaknesses?
- Have you worked for more than one manager? How did you cope?
- How many projects can you handle at a time? Give me an example of when this occurred.
- What tools do you use to keep organized?
- How do you measure your productivity?
- What makes you a good communicator?
- With what types of people do you best get along?
- Tell me about a time you had to go above and beyond the call of duty.

- Tell me about the types of communication you used in your previous position.
- How important was communication with others in your last position?
- What types of communication tools, forms, or documents have you developed?
- What are some communication best practices?
- How have you communicated concerns or criticisms to coworkers? Do you feel you were effective?
- Are there additional considerations when communicating to groups of employees versus individual employees?
- In what instances is written communication better than vocal communication?
- What guidelines should you follow to communicate effectively with your manager?
- What does good customer service mean?
- What efforts have you made in your job to improve customer satisfaction?
- How does your job fit in to your department and company?
- Tell me about a time when you stood up for someone else.
- When have you been most satisfied in your career?

Once I have asked several questions and feel I have elicited enough responses to fairly evaluate the applicant, I conclude the interview with questions that help me ascertain why the candidate wants a virtual position. Examples include:

- How does telecommuting enhance your productivity?
- Describe the tools you use to collaborate and communicate with your managers and peers when working remotely.
- What type of work environment appeals to you most?
- Describe your remote office. (Remember: BYOT.)
- Why do you want to telecommute?

The answers to these questions should indicate the candidate is self-motivated, expects to keep normal business hours, is positioned logistically to work on a remote basis, and can be productive when working independently. Answers along the lines of "Telecommuting reduces my childcare costs," "I work best at night," "I rely on phone and e-mail to communicate," or "If I were offered this position, I would need to set up an Internet connection" are red flags.

A word of advice: Write notes after each interview. Record relevant answers and pertinent details. This will not only help you during the decision-making process, but it will also serve you well if any of your candidates request feedback from you later.

The Selection

After your applicant(s) have completed the interviews, it's time for you to evaluate. Take the time to think about their responses and reflect on which skill sets, experiences, and personalities best lend themselves to your organization's culture, to the position's responsibilities, and to a virtual work arrangement. There is no shortcutting the fact that an applicant must have the core experience for the position, especially a virtual one where a manager's guidance is not necessarily within arm's reach. However, soft skills cannot be ignored either. Trust and communication are critical for a virtual employee to fit in with your team, so be sure to give these equal thought.

CHOOSING VIRTUAL WORKERS FROM WITHIN THE ORGANIZATION

For many organizations, the temptation to allow employees to work from home is stronger than ever. With increased employee engagement, improved productivity, and reduced overhead as byproducts of remote work arrangements, it is no surprise that numerous organizations are migrating to virtual staffing models. But how do you transition employees from a traditional office model setting to a remote working situation? The key is employee selection. Not all employees are well suited for remote work arrangements, and therefore not all employees should be allowed or required to work remotely.

When selecting employees from within your organization to work virtually, you should take care that the employees' personalities fit a virtual worker profile (the four "self" characteristics). Performance reviews should clearly document that the individual is a self-starter, and provide concrete examples of self-motivated, self-disciplined, and self-sufficient behaviors. Do not choose employees who do not have a proven record of results at the office. If someone is performing below par under supervision, you run a high risk of that performance sinking to an all new low without supervision.

In addition—and I cannot stress this particular point enough—you want to make sure the individuals you transition to a virtual work arrangement have strong relationships in place with their particular managers. It is frequently said that employees "join companies and leave managers," and I wholeheartedly believe this. The reality is that when an employee transitions to a virtual work setting, the employee–manager dynamic will change, which can be unnerving. Communication will be different, opportunities to socialize are less frequent, and there will be an increased need for reporting. A remote work arrangement forces a manager to measure, monitor, and reward outcomes differently than "Management by Walking Around." The only way the employee–manager relationship can successfully sustain these changes is when a solid relationship with established trust is already in place.

Case Study: Earning the Privilege to Work Remotely

Choosing virtual workers within an organization is an important task. American Fidelity Assurance, a family-owned organization providing supplemental health insurance benefits and financial services to employees across the U.S., knows firsthand how important this particular point is. In fact, their organization does not hire virtual workers; instead, the company carefully selects virtual employees from within the organization.

Working remotely is an arrangement available to American Fidelity employees who can work effectively in a paperless environment. The company's managers can offer telecommuting at their discretion to employees based on their tasks and work responsibilities. Managers are encouraged to use working virtually as a perk or reward for employees.

"Our telecommuters are excited about the opportunity to telecommute, which naturally leads to being motivated and engaged," said Heather Henshall, HR Project Coordinator of American Fidelity, who is responsible for designing and executing corporate initiatives such as telecommuting and crisis management. "They know it is a perk and they don't want to lose it."[6]

In 2011, American Fidelity had 200 employees in the Oklahoma City corporate headquarters signed up for telecommuting and about 500 field employees already telecommuting. The company, which has been named one of *FORTUNE* magazine's "100 Best Companies to Work For" in America for eight consecutive years, has found telecommuting to be a great retention tool. In fact, the average tenure for an employee is 11 years.

By allowing its staff to work remotely, American Fidelity has demonstrated its commitment to not only engaging and empowering employees, but also retaining them. "If employees aren't engaged, they won't perform at high levels and they won't stay with the company as long," said Henshall.

Employing a virtual workforce has helped American Fidelity keep its customer promise, such as remaining functional even during snowstorms when the physical office closes. Working remotely has also allowed employees to find a healthy work/life balance. For example, employees can run errands on their lunch break or take their children to extracurricular activities.

Most importantly, telecommuting has increased the company's productivity level. Several departments have a large virtual staff, which increases their production and ability to turn around claims quickly. To ensure productivity remains at a high level, working virtually plays an important role in American Fidelity's crisis management plan. Remote workers enable the company to keep their phone lines open and continue to serve their customers at all times.

The statement that American Fidelity is a family company is more than just an expression or an ideal; it's a way of life every single day. Whether giving employees the option to work from home, a coffee shop, or the corporate headquarters, American Fidelity recognizes that its tagline—"Our Family, Dedicated to Yours"— truly encompasses both on-site employees and virtual workers.

TRY A PROBATIONARY PHASE

I believe American Fidelity's strategy in selecting virtual employees from current on-site employees certainly sets the organization up for success. If employers are still hesitant about transitioning employees to a virtual environment, I think having remote workers test the waters in a probationary phase is another effective way to ensure employees will be productive from a distance. Perhaps you engage in a 60- to 90-day trial period, or perhaps you start with a Tuesday, Wednesday, Thursday virtual schedule (this avoids the temptation for the employee to take long weekends). You, as the manager, need to see that the employee can still drive results from a virtual setting, and you can set very simple protocols in place to carefully monitor this, such as requiring the employee to send in a daily report. A probationary phase also communicates to the employee up-front that working from home is a privilege that can be revoked if performance suffers as a result.

Let's face it: Some employees cannot work from home, and you'll discover during this probationary phase if the employee will use the time for errands, laundry, and TV. If this happens, the solution is simple: These folks are not afforded the privilege of working from home. The good news for you is that you have only invested a limited number of days in the endeavor, and the employee is able to return to work and hopefully re-engage.

But a probationary phase is important for the employee, too. Some individuals are surprised to discover that although working from home sounds attractive, the reality is that they prefer an office setting. You want the employee to know that you care about outcomes, not physical location, and therefore the door to return to the office is always open.

Learning curves are important, and in some cases, productivity increases are seen as far out as 18 months after the beginning of a program change, so give yourself and your employees time as you transition them into a remote work setting. Chances are good that if you've drafted the right mix of players for your virtual team, the outcome will be the one that's right for the organization.

CHAPTER 4

WHAT IT ALL BOILS DOWN TO: EMPLOYEE ENGAGEMENT

The most successful workforces, whether collocated or virtual, are those that employ the best individuals. The most important quality of successful virtual employees is engagement. A culture of engagement across locations fosters incredible business outcomes.

WHAT IS EMPLOYEE ENGAGEMENT?

Employee engagement is the connection employees feel with the organization for which they work. Engagement promotes a magnetic culture that draws talented employees to the workplace, empowers them, and sustains an environment in which they are less likely to leave. A magnetic culture is built on a foundation of engaged employees.

Engaged employees possess an intellectual commitment and emotional bond (pride, passion, enthusiasm) to their employer and an eagerness to exert extra discretionary effort and creativity, as well as a willingness to accept some personal ownership for their own level of engagement, all leading to maximized outcomes for themselves, for the organization, and for customers. When an organization consists of engaged employees, positive organizational outcomes will result. The ROE (Return on engagement) is tremendous.

ROE: RETURN ON ENGAGEMENT

Most of you have heard of return on investment (ROI), but what about return on engagement, or ROE? ROE is the financial effect engagement has on an organization. HR Solutions' Research Institute has found that engagement leads to an overall lower bottom line and a multitude of constructive business results.

It is imperative that virtual managers understand how and why engagement contributes to positive business outcomes. In recognizing this contribution, managers, leadership, and employees alike will be more inclined to work to increase engagement among team members. Managing engagement truly is an important first step in becoming the best virtual manager and maintaining the most successful virtual employees.

HOW ENGAGEMENT AFFECTS YOUR BOTTOM LINE

Increased Performance

HR Solutions' Research Institute has found a positive, nearly perfect correlation between engagement and performance.

Virtual employees who are engaged and committed to their organization will remain dedicated to high-quality performance despite the distance between them, their "head office," their manager, their coworkers, and their end-customer. This is a somewhat intuitive claim: When one is interested in and dedicated to what he is doing, he will be more likely to exert extra effort to provide the best result, regardless of direct supervision, distance, or outside factors. Additionally, he will go above and beyond to provide innovative ideas to the organization, consistently thinking outside the box.

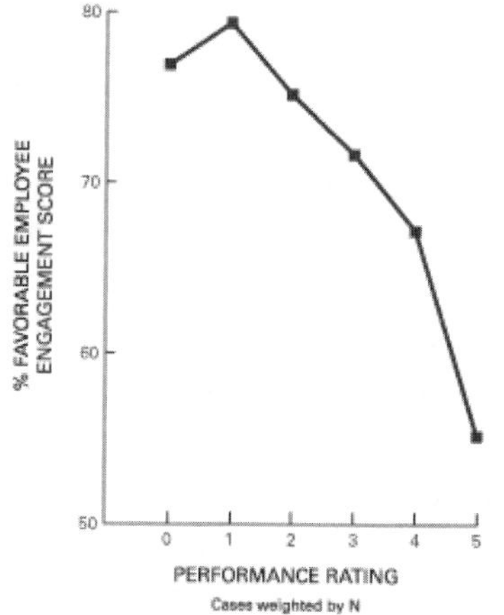

Performance Rating	N Observations	% Favorable Mean All Survey Dimensions
O NA	6772	76.92
1 BEST	13718	79.37
2	44100	75.19
3	49757	71.66
4	2965	67.21
5 WORST	556	55.22
Total	117868	73.99

Linkage between performance evaluations and engagement.

If remote workers enjoy the majority of what they do, they will contribute more to the organization regardless of where they are located. They will go the extra mile to bridge the detachment between themselves, their managers, and their coworkers. Extra effort could range from creating very high-quality work to designing an innovative way of nurturing culture and connections among virtual employees. Engaged employees are more likely to go above and beyond, contributing to more comprehensive and creative work.

Engaged individuals also tend to take on more work, accomplishing greater amounts in the same time as other, less-engaged employees. Virtual team members engaged in the organization and its *purpose* are much more actively aware of what needs to be accomplished, and gladly volunteer to contribute as much as they can. When a greater amount of work is completed, the number of extra employees organizations need to hire may be reduced as a result. So, through building virtual employee engagement, managers can save a lot on hiring costs. Virtual employee engagement acts much like a magnet, easily drawing top talent into the organization and lowering recruiting costs.

Engaged employees mean better performance and more high-quality output. When an organization produces superior results, it will establish a reputation as a thriving and exceptional business. With such a strong reputation, employees will remain engaged in the incomparable culture of the organization.

Retention

HR Solutions' Research Institute has found that engaged employees are 3.5 times more likely to remain with their organization. Engagement fosters an emotional connection with numerous aspects of an employee's job, and with this inspiration of heart, employees have less reason to search elsewhere for a new position. Research shows that virtual employees are more satisfied than their in-office coworkers.[1] As such, implementing and leveraging virtual work policies will contribute to higher retention.

It costs 138 percent of actual wages to hire and train a new employee rather than retain an old one.[2] The high cost of filling a position includes the time current employees spend reviewing resumes, interviewing potential job candidates, hiring individuals, and training them once they are hired. It takes eight weeks, on average, to hire a new employee.[3] It is time-consuming and costly to obtain new team members; organizational costs can be greatly reduced by retaining employees.

Training costs and time may be even more exacerbated for the virtual workforce: When employees are located at a distance, it is often harder to train them on given tasks. Consider a new hire who is being trained in an office. This individual can shadow an employee who has been with the organization for a while, thus gleaning information through hands-on activities. Virtual employees, however, largely must try and observe from a distance. They cannot necessarily view the project specifics. In addition, technology limits what can be done in the training realm. It is better to retain existing virtual employees than to continually hire replacement individuals who must undergo the new-hire process from a distance.

ENGAGED EMPLOYEES = SATISFIED AND LOYAL CUSTOMERS

Engaged employees are linked to satisfied customers with a correlation coefficient of 0.85. This positive correlation indicates that as the number of engaged employees within an organization increases, the number of satisfied customers also increases. Engaged employees put forth more effort to provide exceptional customer service, thus contributing to an overall better outcome for customers. A culture of engagement thus leads to satisfied customers, which in turn means greater profits.

Case Study: 7-Eleven *Undercover Boss*

Undercover Boss, a popular reality show on CBS in early 2012, is a weekly TV show that follows senior-level executives as they leave their corporate office, disguise their identity, and work alongside line-level employees to evaluate the inner workings of their organization. Undercover bosses such as Joseph DePinto, president and CEO of 7-Eleven, often serve as virtual managers, as they do not necessarily interact with their employees regularly. One particular 7-Eleven location consistently sold more coffee than any other location. When going undercover there, DePinto found customers were drawn to the location not necessarily by its products, but rather based on their interactions with Dolores, an affable employee who knew many of her customers by name. Her dedication and commitment to the customer, going above and beyond to get to know them rather than simply fulfilling their order, attracts customers to the store. Dolores is a perfect example of an engaged employee leading to satisfied customers. With the positive experience they have, these satisfied customers will likely return.

When customers are satisfied with their experiences, they are more likely to become recurrent consumers, and customer loyalty drives profitability and growth. A 5-percent increase in customer loyalty can boost profits by 25 to 85 percent.[4] Not only will satisfied customers remain loyal, thus increasing profits, it also costs less to attract new customers. On average, it costs five times more to attract a new customer than to retain a repeat customer.[5] Bottom-line costs of attracting new customers are thus reduced when satisfied customers are retained.

Additionally, satisfied customers mean positive reviews. Customers are likely to share their opinions with others, and can thereby attract or discourage others from frequenting your organization, depending on their reviews. In the remote world, customers who interact with virtual employees are often exceptionally Internet-savvy, as they often communicate online with remote workers. When they have a review to post, they will be more likely to tweet the review or post it to social media. As the whole foundation of social media is to share, the review will spread quickly and immediately. Even in the real (non-virtual) world, the spread of opinions, known as the multiplier effect, can be devastating to an organization. Studies have shown that, on average, one unhappy customer tells 10 people about their poor experience; those 10 people, in turn, tell at least five other individuals about that experience. Thus, one poor customer experience can lead to lost business with 61 people in all. Social media and "sharing" provide potential for an even greater dissemination of reviews. If you multiply these figures by the potential lost business, the results are staggering. Thus, social media and Internet company reviews have created the Multiplier Effect on Steroids. For virtual managers, it is *fundamental* to foster a culture of engagement; the more positive reviews you can provide, the more chance you have of overcoming negative reviews (and hopefully wiping them out altogether).

REPUTATION: CREATING NET PROMOTERS AND BRAND CHAMPIONS

Employee branding is the overall perception (thinking and feeling) the employee has about his or her experience working within an organization. Further, employee branding reflects how well the organization's vision and strategy are "branded" into the psyche of the employee. The more positively employees feel about the company, the more likely they will be to spread positive reviews to customers. Such was the genesis for the entire "net promoter" concept first introduced in 2003 by Satmetrix, Bain & Company, and Fred Reichheld. Getting your virtual employees emotionally and intellectually committed to your organization and its brands will encourage them to actively promote both your employment brand and your product/service brand to prospective employees and customers. This is the reason that any employee engagement survey worth its salt will include sentences like:

- I would proudly recommend this organization as a great place to work.
- I would proudly recommend our organization's products and services to others.

The financial impact of creating these "brand champions" is overwhelming, as well as infectious, spurring further revenue growth and enviable profitability. In fact, companies with higher employee engagement levels have 2.6 times greater earnings per share than organizations with average or lackluster engagement levels.[6]

If actively engaged employees are an organization's biggest fans, then disengaged employees would be the people throwing tomatoes at the stage. Disengaged employees can provide detrimental PR for an organization. After all, most people expect employees to be the most qualified to speak about the organization for which they work. In fact, some job search candidates have even begun contacting employees at organizations prior to applying or interviewing in order to feel out the organization via its employees' opinions. In recent years, large online forums such as Yelp and Glassdoor have sprouted up on the Web for customers and employees alike to review various organizations.

Imagine you read an online review from a previous employee stating the organization you're considering working for is unorganized, the employees and management are more concerned about profits than customer service, and the data the organization supplies is not accurate. Would you be likely to support that organization? If an organization's employees only have bad things to say, people will take their comments seriously and likely adopt the same opinion without further investigating the facts.

If virtual managers are managing in such a way that they are accepting ambivalence and tolerating the toxic effects of actively disengaged employees, then they are much more likely to see these negative comments on the Web. All great talent-management and talent-attraction efforts can be promptly undermined and rendered useless by such public postings, so wise virtual managers will actively manage their disengaged employees *out* of the organization because these are the very people that want to say negative things about the brand. Smart virtual managers will also regularly check these sites not only to discover what comments are out there, but also to encourage the best, most engaged workers to publically post their awesome sentiments about the company.

On the other hand, engaged employees will go out of their way to attract customers and keep them satisfied. They will follow up with phone calls or e-mails, despite being across the globe. Actively engaged team members will go above and beyond to meet their customers' needs, even if it means working late due to a time-zone conflict. They are also apt to believe "the customer *always* comes first."

INCREASED PROFITS

Organizations that maximize employee engagement outperform their competitors on operational budget, revenue, and even stock performance. Increased productivity and devotion to the organization contribute to greater discretionary effort, which can be leveraged for better business outcomes. Additionally, customer satisfaction and loyalty resulting from interactions with engaged employees will contribute to greater and more widespread business, thus increasing profits.

REDUCED ABSENTEEISM

A study of employees throughout various countries found that significant numbers of individuals admit to calling in sick to work when they are not really ill. In the United States, 52 percent of those surveyed reported doing so.[7] HR Solutions' Research Institute found that when organizations increase engagement among their employees, they report 80 percent less absenteeism. As with anything in life, if you are not involved or invested, you are less likely to want to participate. This is true for an organization as well: The more involved employees are in what they are doing, the more likely they are to want to contribute on a daily basis. With a decrease in absenteeism, bottom-line costs for the organization can be greatly reduced. As mentioned in Chapter 1, the estimated per-employee cost for absences is $789 per year.[8] Thus, when organizations see fewer unscheduled absences, they will report greater savings, leading to further return on engagement.

SAFETY

Engagement is also correlated with safety. If an employee is dedicated to her organization, she will likely rise above the call of duty to make it a safe place to work. In a manufacturing organization, for example, if an engaged employee sees a spill, she will be more willing to go out of her way to clean it up, as she recognizes it as a safety hazard. A disengaged employee may simply ignore the spill, figuring someone else will handle it accordingly. Additionally, engaged employees will likely put forth discretionary effort to develop ideas that will make the organization even safer.

POLICY COMPLIANCE

Engaged employees show greater compliance with company policy. They go out of their way to understand each aspect of their organization's policies, and thus are more informed when it comes to handling any issues that arise. They will go above and beyond to abide by the organization's protocols, recognizing that there is a reason these policies are in place. Their loyalty to the organization will help hold them accountable to following the correct protocols.

In all of the aforementioned ways, engaged employees contribute to increased profits and cut bottom-line costs. The best virtual managers will recognize the importance of engagement, and will work with their team to create a team of engaged virtual employees, despite the physical separation and related challenges.

SATISFACTION VS. ENGAGEMENT

In the past, management at many organizations has been largely concerned with measuring the satisfaction levels of employees, but satisfaction is simply a mood or opinion pertaining to the organization, whereas *engagement* refers to actual behaviors and investment. Engagement takes satisfaction to a whole new level. Satisfaction is "shiny, happy people,

holding hands and laughing" (to quote an R.E.M. song), whereas engagement takes these individuals and pushes them to make a difference. Satisfaction is contentment with the organization, whereas engagement is taking the initiative to make the organization *exceptional*. The best, most innovative outcomes result from engagement. The most successful virtual managers will recognize the difference between satisfaction and engagement, and go beyond simply satisfying their virtual employees. Engaged virtual employees will create the absolute best virtual organization.

Building engagement begins with identifying each employee's engagement level and then working individually to improve engagement throughout the organization.

THE THREE BUCKETS OF EMPLOYEE ENGAGEMENT

Individuals fall into three "Buckets of Engagement" based on their connection to the organization for which they work. The bucket into which an individual falls largely determines his contribution to the organization. When employees work virtually, it is imperative to determine into which bucket they fall; doing so will permit virtual managers to tailor policies and implement practices to create the best virtual employees.

The three Buckets of Engagement are:

- Actively engaged.
- Ambivalent.
- Actively disengaged.

Actively Engaged

Actively engaged employees are the team members who will contribute the greatest amount to your organization, regardless of their location. These team members are exceptionally dedicated to the organization for which they work. They feel a strong emotional bond to the company. Employees in this category tend to regularly exert discretionary effort during their projects. They are largely driven by their job content, as long as they have been put in a position to do what they do best and utilize their special skills and abilities.

Furthermore, engaged team members working remotely will often begin work prior to their established schedule, despite knowing they will not be seen by management—rather, they do it for themselves. Actively engaged individuals will also continue working longer than they are required to, so as to accomplish tasks they need to finish. They thoroughly enjoy the majority of their work. In addition, these employees are role models to their peers, finding ways to encourage others in the organization to strive to be the best they can be despite being miles away. They are optimistic and have positive outlooks overall. These employees often offer rave reviews of their organization and could be considered cheerleaders for their company and its brand.

Employees in the actively engaged bucket tend to complete work on time and with exceptional quality. They often have organized work spaces. They are known to go above and beyond the call of duty, and provide innovative ideas. Actively engaged employees have a strong desire to be part of the value and outcomes of the organization. Personal qualities possessed by these employees include self-motivation, loyalty to the organization, and being an inspiration to others, all three of which make for the ideal virtual employee.

Actively engaged employees are those who are likely to understand exactly how working virtually will benefit the company. They will present a comprehensive outline of the amount of work they contribute, and how the organization benefits from a virtual work policy. Engaged employees in offices separate from their manager will detail how they are contributing and realize they need to go above and beyond without their manager present. Engagement among virtual employees will be obvious through a focus on overall outcomes, rather than on the individual (for example, "The work I accomplish while outside of the office will be more thoroughly researched, providing more validity to the organization" as opposed to "I can do more work at home").

Examples of Actively Engaged:

Sue works from an office in England and her direct supervisor works in the United States. Despite the distance, she consistently arrives early to work, regardless of the fact that her manager is not there to observe her. She is always prepared for video and conference calls, and often presents new and innovative ideas to advance the organization. She volunteers for extra projects, and encourages other team members to contribute their ideas as well.

Jane works on-site with clients multiple days each week, rarely frequenting the main headquarters of her organization. She never fails to arrive early, and is completely focused on the best outcomes for her customers. She will always answer any questions posed by clients, even if it means spending extra time driving to the main office to consult directly with coworkers.

Jim works remotely twice a week. During the days he is out of the office, he regularly wakes early in order to get a head start on his projects for the day. He responds to e-mails in a timely fashion, and is more than willing to take phone calls if something needs to be clarified. If he is requested to be in the office on a day he originally planned to work virtually, he is happy to make the effort, rearranging his schedule to accommodate any changes.

Ambivalent

Ambivalent employees are primarily motivated by the desire for a paycheck. These individuals are the remote employees most likely to get lost in the virtual world, as their feelings of disconnect will discourage them from establishing a connection to the organization and exerting effort to remain involved. They are known to do only the work assigned to them, rarely exerting extra effort for the good of the organization. Simply put, they are doing just enough to get by. In meetings or on conference calls, when volunteers are requested to take on extra projects, ambivalent employees are not likely to proffer their name or verbally agree to contribute. Employees in this category frequently start work exactly on time and quit promptly when the clock says their day is over. They are not apt to go the extra mile. They often do everything they can to blend in to the background by responding to e-mails or community voice mails only when explicitly asked to do so. Ambivalent employees are habitually uninvolved in the organization and lack spirit or enthusiasm for the goals and values of their company. Their work spaces do not look lived in, reflecting the disconnect employees in this category feel. Additionally, ambivalent team members often feel unappreciated and insignificant.

Examples of Ambivalent:

Joe works at a distance four days a week. On the days when he is working remotely, he tends to sleep in, waking up just in time to log into the system, and shuts his computer down promptly at the agreed-upon end time. He does only enough work each day to meet deadlines established by his supervisor. If the deadline is not for a few days, Joe will likely not make progress on the project during his time working remotely, as he will "finish it in the office." If he finishes a project early, Joe will wait until something else is assigned; he will likely not use the free time he has to think of creative and fresh ideas for his company, but rather to catch up on personal items, or do nothing at all.

Matt works in a small office in Italy, with his manager located in the global headquarters in China. Matt is always copied on e-mail chains with coworkers, but he tends to only respond when asked a question directly. If his peers are discussing a new project, he will likely not volunteer to contribute. On conference calls, Matt remains on the line, listening but rarely providing his opinion.

Actively Disengaged

Actively disengaged employees feel little if any connection to the organization. They tend to have a negative energy about their jobs, and put forth very minimal effort. Disengaged employees never volunteer for extra work, and the projects they do complete are often poor in quality, thus requiring re-work. Because the actively disengaged employee refuses to correct any mistakes, as she either does not want to admit and be accountable for the work's shoddy quality in the first place or simply doesn't want to work, the re-work often falls to others.

Employees in the disengaged bucket are regularly disorganized in their duties, sometimes even forgetting what needs to be done. In the on-site world, these employees are referred to as "water cooler malcontents," because they can often be found near the water cooler, complaining to anyone who will listen. In the virtual world, these employees are those sending joke e-mails, surreptitiously gossiping on phone calls, or complaining to anyone available instead of working.

Furthermore, disengaged virtual employees are more likely to sleep in instead of waking up to get an early start on their projects. Additionally, they show a lack of respect for their coworkers by not responding to e-mails in a timely fashion, missing conference calls, refusing to return voice mails, or bothering their peers in the office because the manager will never see this occurring. They will often stop working before the day is complete or spend time on personal obligations rather than work that needs to be accomplished each day.

Disengaged team members are the remote employees who thrive under the idea that management is across the world, unaware of what hours they are keeping. They often believe, "When the cat's away, the mice will play." They will likely slack off because their manager is not present. Their ideas behind working virtually are "me-focused," rather than focused on the outcomes for the organization. They tend to do less work at home than they did in the office, and as these individuals don't get much accomplished in the office anyway, the amount they do at home will be very minimal.

Actively disengaged remote employees are known for their *virtual absenteeism*. Virtual absenteeism occurs when the remote employee (not surprisingly, most often the actively disengaged employee) logs on, pretending to work, only to log off mentally from the employer and its purpose in order to do some other activity completely unrelated to work. Virtual absenteeism is costing organizations and managers dearly.

One best practice to eliminate this cost is to elicit the assistance of the IT department; should you suspect that virtual absenteeism is occurring with one of your remote workers, act on it. This goes back to the cornerstone of success for the virtual team talked about previously: trust. Simply ask your trusted IT professional to verify that the remote worker is showing computer key strokes that indicate he or she is actually working, as opposed to just being logged on. Importantly, the aforementioned best practice suggestion should only be done when you have a strong suspicion or evidence that the employee is virtually absent; that way you will not undermine the great trust you have built with the other people you manage. You would never want any of those people thinking that you are spying on them.

Examples of Actively Disengaged:

Bob meets daily with clients at their places of business, while his main office is located in a neighboring state. He considers his car his office, as he is always in it, traveling from customer to customer. When viewing the inside of his car, you can see papers strewn about and coffee spilled on documents, and it looks as though he forgot to throw out that sandwich he had for lunch—three days ago. He often does not know the answers to questions posed by clients. Instead of offering to find the answers, he simply says, "I don't know. That's not part of my job."

Jennifer works in an office in Ohio; her manager is located in Texas. She arrives late to work, figuring her supervisor will never know. They conduct their meetings via video conferencing. Jennifer's manager has learned to schedule meetings plenty in advance, as Jennifer is always late. She arrives unprepared, and barely contributes to the conversation.

Twice a week, John works out of his home office. During these days, he wakes up late and uses plenty of time before actually sitting down to accomplish work-related projects. He takes long breaks throughout the day, running personal errands or meeting up with friends. After finishing a project (late), even when he has time left on the clock, John tends to head to the gym or out to eat, rather than preparing for the next day.

Jen, a virtual manager who works in an office with five employees while managing other employees across the world, is "virtually absent." She comes into work, turns her chair toward the window, places her coat on the back, and leaves a half-filled cup of soda on her desk. In this way, she can make her five on-site employees believe she's at work and simply stepped out for a moment, when in actuality, she is taking the morning off. Although unlikely, if necessary, she knows she can answer phone calls or e-mails from her virtual employees, as they will never know where she is located, especially if her calls get re-routed to her cell phone. If managers can do this while in the same office as other employees, imagine how detrimental it would be if they no longer have to put up any front, and can simply not work, knowing they will never be observed.

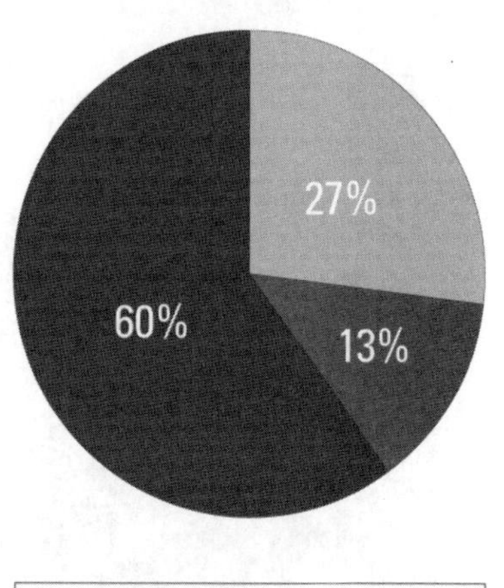

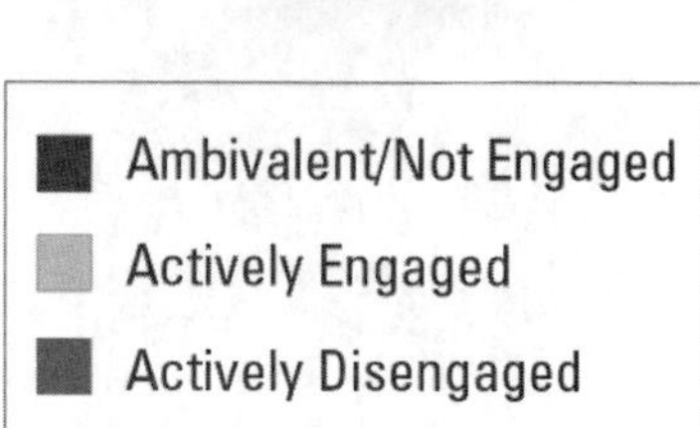

INTERNATIONAL STATISTICS ON EMPLOYEE ENGAGEMENT

The numbers don't lie: 73 percent of the workforce is not engaged. This is a wake-up call for organizations, regardless of industry or size, to develop ongoing strategies to create engaged workplaces and continually seek employee feedback to measure levels of engagement and affect positive change.

THE SPREAD OF ENGAGEMENT

Each individual's engagement level affects the way he interacts with other team members. Engagement levels often feed off each other. Despite not necessarily being in close proximity, individuals in the virtual environment will still affect each other.

Even through the distance, employees are strongly influenced by the individuals with whom they are interacting. If ambivalent employees are communicating with actively engaged employees, they will be more likely to take a positive stance on the organization. However, if ambivalent employees are interacting with disengaged employees, they will likely adopt the attitudes of these individuals. Recognizing how engagement levels spread is an important first step for effective virtual managers to reduce the spread of disengagement.

Importantly, despite not being actively engaged, ambivalent employees can be considered diamonds in the rough. They need a little time and molding, but eventually they can become actively engaged employees.

Managers should consider the drivers of engagement in order to fully understand why employees fall into the ambivalent category. As clearly suggested in Chapter 1, conversations with ambivalent employees about their particular drivers and detractors will help leadership comprehend how best to engage them.

Disengaged employees are the cancer of an organization. Their attitudes and behaviors will literally infect those in contact with them, significantly decreasing their coworkers' engagement levels. Ambivalent employees are especially susceptible, and placing them in close contact with disengaged employees can cause the disease of disengagement to spread quickly throughout an organization.

Exposure to other team members will also contribute to changes in ambivalent employees' engagement levels. Despite the physical separation in the remote world, engagement is evident in e-mail and virtual practices. Disengagement can be conveyed in an e-mail by a lack of proofreading, a disregard to detail, and/or a flighty tone. Speaking of tone, both the manager's tone and the remote employee's tone play a far greater role in whether the relationship is successful compared to the more traditional on-site workplace relationship: In the absence of physical cues such as facial expressions and hand gestures, virtual managers and employees have a greater propensity to be more sensitive to, and even pre-judge, the tone of the other party. In addition, snippiness, evasiveness, or even long sighs of despair are likely to speak volumes of negativity to the recipient. Thus, successful organizations with virtual workforces will address this important topic during new-employee orientation as well as the training given to the virtual manager.

In addition, a lack of urgency or unresponsiveness to e-mails and phone calls may reflect an "I don't care" mentality common among disengaged employees. When ambivalent employees encounter these e-mails, they may be likely to adopt these practices, pouring themselves into the disengaged bucket.

Disengaged employees tend to look for individuals who will share their unhappiness, as misery loves company. Sad but true, actively disengaged employees will often aggressively seek out a new remote employee on the new employee's very first day on the job, with the noxious purpose of infecting her with comments that begin with "Let me tell you what it is *really* like to work here...." Because ambivalent employees are often on the fence, disengaged employees are likely to draw them into the disengaged bucket. Even without being in the presence of a disengaged employee, ambivalent employees are at risk of being drawn into the disengaged circle. Disengaged employees can be seen as the small hole in the side of a boat, which can continue to get bigger if permitted to, eventually leading to the sinking of the ship.

One team member's disengagement will likely contribute to frustration from others. If disengaged employees refuse to respond to e-mails, or wait days before replying, ambivalent and even engaged employees may become frustrated and disillusioned. After all, it's incredibly hard to complete a group project when not everyone is contributing their part. It's frustrating enough to not get a response in a responsible amount of time, and if employees feel that management is not doing something to correct this problem, they are likely to become disengaged as well. Tolerance of disengagement will inevitably become completely disheartening to your very best virtual workers, leading them to question why they have to pull the load for, and put up with, such poor and destructive coworkers. Notably, these "A Players" will also begin to question the competence and managerial skills of the virtual manager if such disengagement remains unchecked and is not managed.

On the other side, engaged individuals will likely convey a tone of gratitude and excitement when writing e-mails to coworkers. They will reach out to individuals who need extra support, aware of the contribution this support will provide to the entire organization. They will return phone calls in a timely manner, and prepare materials well in advance, recognizing the amount of time it takes to transfer information between locations. They will develop bonds with individuals across locales, in an effort to create an effective, engaged culture and lessen the amount of detachment. When ambivalent employees receive e-mails or calls from engaged employees, they will be more apt to mimic and embrace a similar passion for the organization, thus developing an inclination toward the engaged bucket.

Additionally contributing to the spread of engagement is the fact that people's opinions of us matter. In other words, we have a strong desire to be liked. Consider an employee who starts a new job as a remote worker. He begins as an actively engaged employee, responding promptly to e-mails, returning phone calls, and developing amazing plans to connect various offices across the organization. However, as time wears on, he does not receive recognition, praise, or even acknowledgment of his initiatives. He is unable to convince others to join his efforts and has a hard time bridging the distance between locations, as his less-engaged coworkers eventually stop responding to his e-mails, voice mails, and questions.

Finally, team members copy him on an e-mail explaining how his responsiveness and innovation are making them look unproductive and indifferent. In order to fit in, the formerly engaged employee begins to cut back on his performance, becoming another ambivalent employee within the organization.

Leadership may not notice an actively engaged employee's slow descent to ambivalence unfolding, especially given the distance between virtual managers and virtual employees. The engagement "slippage" scenario here underscores the importance of recognition as a key driver of engagement for the remote employee, to be utilized and leveraged consistently by the virtual manager. A great best practice of exceptional virtual managers is to establish regular check-ins with their A Players to ensure sustained engagement and prevent any erosion. Another best practice incredible virtual managers employ is to institute regular check-ins on themselves, assessing whether they are spending far too much time coaching and hoping for improvement from their problem employees, which is sapping the time and attention they could be giving to their top talent. Such an honest self-assessment will prompt the best virtual managers to recalibrate their time and attention accordingly.

To provide a concrete illustration of the spread of engagement, let's think of an organization like a boat about to embark on a long cruise. Engaged employees are those individuals on the boat who are thoroughly enjoying their time. Ambivalent employees are those sitting around, not taking advantage of all the cruise has to offer. Disengaged employees are the people moping in the corner, or complaining about the heat and noise. Very few people would prefer to take a journey on a boat filled with ambivalent or disengaged individuals. Further, imagine rowing a boat in which most everyone is rowing hard in the correct direction, but some are remaining still and not contributing, and others are rowing backward. In a boat such as this, forward movement is bound to be limited, and forward-rowers must work harder to compensate for the lack of effort from others.

Potential employees will be more likely to come aboard a boat if the individuals already aboard are enthusiastic, having a good time, and advancing in the right direction. As such, establishing a culture of engagement will increase the chances outsiders will see your organization as a good place to take a ride, thus allowing you to attract top talent and loyal customers. It is a wonderful cycle to witness: Attracting top talent contributes to a culture of engagement, which in turn allows you to attract more top talent and loyal, repeat customers.

Get the right people on board and the wrong ones off before you embark on a successful business journey.

THE JOINT MODEL OF EMPLOYEE ENGAGEMENT

For years, great managers have worked to build employee engagement from their side of the equation. When an employee complained that her manager wasn't communicating effectively, the manager worked to improve his communication skills. When an employee said she would be more engaged if she received more recognition, the manager tried to thank the employee more often.

For virtual managers, this type of action and response is not always possible. Without in-person clues (body language) from the employee, it is harder for managers to tell that something is bothering him. In addition, employees who work remotely may feel less comfortable speaking with their managers, and therefore less likely to feel comfortable bringing up workplace problems. Virtual managers can sometimes feel clueless about how to engage their staff, and therefore point resources in the wrong direction.

Relying on the manager to respond to employee issues can help to increase employee engagement, but it presents an oxymoron: How can you increase employee engagement without involving the employee? The answer is: the Joint Model of Employee Engagement.

Managers and *organizations* have been tasked for decades with building engagement among their *employees*, which actually causes a lopsided look at employee engagement: Organizations rarely saw the results they wanted from their engagement initiatives because they were only focusing on half of the solution. Why has the responsibility for employee engagement been squarely and solely placed on the shoulders of management? Why has no one questioned the lopsided and unhealthy nature of this approach? For years this unbalanced approach has created very paternalistic expectations and outcomes. Employees are literally and figuratively leaning back in their chairs, pointing to the manager, and saying things like "Do this and I'll become more engaged," when really the employees themselves should be involved in the process of building, and accepting some ownership for their own engagement.

This lopsided perspective was well described by one of HR Solutions' clients in healthcare, Rick Lovering, the vice president of human resources and Organizational Development at AtlantiCare in New Jersey: "I know of no other healthy relationship that rests on a pillar of one-way responsibility and communication. My relationship with my spouse is a two-way street. My connection with my children rests on two-way rights. My association with my church shares joint ownership. One's relationship with their community should be equally a joint stewardship. Why should it be different with the employer/employee relationship?"

Indeed, a very good point. Why would we want to set up the management/employee relationship as a one-way street—destined to either fail or produce half-hearted outcomes?

In virtual workplaces, managers and employees must learn to share the responsibility for building employee engagement. Through this two-pronged approach, organizations that previously saw their engagement levels hover in mediocrity have seen engagement scores increase by leaps and bounds. To truly increase employee engagement, organizations should follow HR Solutions' Engagement Philosophy:

- EMPOWER employees to learn their own level of engagement.
- ENCOURAGE employees to take ownership of their engagement.
- EDUCATE managers and employees that working together will build higher individual and organizational engagement levels.

Introducing the Concept of Engagement

Enthusiasm is one of the most powerful engines of success. When you do a thing, do it with your might. Put your whole soul into it. Stamp it with your own personality. Be active, be energetic, be enthusiastic and faithful, and you will accomplish your object. Nothing great was ever achieved without enthusiasm.

—Ralph Waldo Emerson

Even though employee engagement is a rather widespread idea among management, many employees have never heard the term before, or may have heard of engagement but do not fully understand what it is or what it means. Before employees can focus on building their own engagement, they must first know what engagement is. The best way to do so is through example, as virtual employees who are new to the workforce may never have seen an actively engaged employee in person.

To explain the concept of engagement, I like to use the example of two employees from my marketing department, Amelia and Kristina. We were in the middle of planning for a large educational event, and these employees received a notification from our system every time a new person registered for the event. Upon returning to the office after a couple of days on the road, I kept hearing horns through the wall of my office. I went out to see what was going on, and it turned out Amelia and Kristina had found little party noisemakers from a recent in-office celebration, and had decided to show their excitement for our upcoming event by blowing their horns to alert the entire office every time someone registered for the event. Their enthusiasm for the event and their jobs was palpable, and truly showed the marks of employee engagement.

After educating employees about the concept of engagement, it is important to show them the benefits they can personally see from becoming engaged, rather than just organizational benefits. Employee benefits from improved engagement include:

- Getting the recognition they deserve.
- Helping develop a clear career path to promotions and advancement.
- Making their job more interesting.
- Learning how to work with a difficult manager and how to manage their manager.
- Helping their managers understand them.
- Procuring the resources they need to do their job and do it well.

By showing employees what they have to gain from becoming engaged, employees are much more likely to buy in to the process and care about their personal engagement level.

Getting the Discussion Started

Once employees understand employee engagement and its importance in the workplace, it is important for managers to initiate a discussion with employees about their personal level of engagement. In my experience as a manager, I've found the best way to open a dialogue about employee engagement is to sit down for a one-on-one meeting with each employee. For virtual managers, this type of discussion is best conducted via video chat in order to assess nonverbal cues from the employee. My best practice is to include this conversation in the employee's performance evaluation. During this time, managers usually talk solely about performance. However, because engagement is linked so closely with performance, it makes sense to discuss both.

I personally don't understand why more managers don't include a discussion of employee engagement in their performance evaluations. A recent study by HR Solutions' Research Institute revealed that no more than 5 percent of the performance reviews conducted by managers have a dialogue between the manager and the employee about the employee's personal engagement level. To me, that is astounding. When you stop and think about all of the time, money, and attention given to the concept of employee engagement, it is truly remarkable that the topic gets such scant airtime *when it matters most*. Few managers are discussing engagement directly with their employees, despite the fact that only 34 percent of HR professionals currently believe employee morale and engagement are strong at their organization.[9] These days you would be hard-pressed to pick up any human resources–related trade journal or magazine and not see an article on employee engagement, yet so few managers take the time to proactively ask employees about what might be contributing to, or detracting from, their engagement level. Extraordinary virtual managers have already recognized and valued such a healthy discussion, especially because this discourse can contribute so nicely to achieving success with the aforementioned virtual team issues surrounding trust and solitary detachment.

Talented virtual managers will make such an important engagement conversation inescapable. How? It is as simple as adding it as a section in the actual performance appraisal form used for performance reviews. Take a look at the performance review forms used by your organization; more than likely, there is no section prompting a meaningful conversation about engagement. It is high time that organizations update both their thinking and their forms. Sadly, not doing so robs managers of the awesome opportunity to show that they care about the employee's engagement level. Just think about how positive a message is being sent to the virtual employee when a manager makes comments and asks questions like:

- "One of the things I care a lot about is your level of job engagement. I'd like to talk to you about this because I would really like to help support you and how engaged you are in your job."
- "What do you find really excites and engages you in your job? What do you like doing the most?"
- "Is there anything that you find is detracting from your engagement level? Anything I can do to help?"

The last two questions illustrate just how easy it is to have the talk with the employee, as well as how simple it is to genuinely show that you care about her. The last two quotes also illuminate just how simple the resulting actions are: Feed the virtual worker more of what she loves and make every attempt to remove as much of the engagement detractors as possible.

Furthermore, a discussion about engagement can reveal a number of factors that may be hampering an employee's performance that the manager never would have heard about otherwise. In addition, during a performance review, an open dialogue has already been established, allowing remote employees who may feel uncomfortable speaking with their managers about workplace issues to voice their opinions freely.

PEER

An excellent way for employees to find out their true engagement level is through PEER, the Personal Employee Engagement Report. PEER revolutionizes the relationship between employees and managers by putting engagement in the hands of employees. PEER is an optional and fully confidential report that not only highlights the employee's level for engagement (actively engaged, ambivalent, or actively disengaged) but also makes useful subject-specific suggestions on how an employee can enhance his own engagement in the workplace. Suggestions for specific action steps are based on how an employee responds to certain items in the survey.

For example, if an employee scores unfavorably in response to the item "My supervisor encourages my career growth," her PEER report would provide ideas for improving that career dimension, which is also the number-two engagement driver.

Some suggestions are:

"Discuss the importance of senior manager visibility with your supervisor. Identify which senior leaders you and the work group would like to see more frequently and ask your supervisor to see if these senior leaders could visit the department."

"Communicate individual and team accomplishments to management/leadership team to improve recognition and awareness of contributions to the organization's strategic goals."

PEER helps employees receive personalized, actionable advice for increasing engagement. It is an excellent tool for supporting the process of joint ownership. If you would like to receive a free trial of PEER to better understand your personal engagement level, please visit *www.hrsolutionsinc.com/peer.cfm*.

I ask all of my direct reports to bring their PEER reports to their performance reviews so that we can discuss the issues that are holding them back from being fully engaged. This dialogue helps to identify a number of issues I wouldn't have known about otherwise, including career growth, feedback, recognition, and coworker relations.

One of these talks led to a new bonus program for the direct report who felt there simply was not enough financial recognition for his job-related efforts specific to revenue generation.

Another employee let me know that she wasn't receiving enough feedback, which was holding her back from being fully engaged. We were then perfectly set up to have a discussion about her issue with feedback, as well as ways both of us can work on improving feedback. For example, as her manager, I will now pay special attention to providing feedback on the work I receive from her. However, if she is not satisfied with the amount of feedback I provide, it is her responsibility to ask for additional feedback or clarification. We have now created a balanced relationship in which both of us feel comfortable discussing her feedback needs as well as her personal engagement.

My favorite outcome regarding having the PEER talk with my direct reports was something I learned from the manager of our quality data services department. Although the PEER report she received (remember that this is her own Personal Employee Engagement Report) showed her to be an actively engaged employee, when prompted to share what might be detracting from her engagement, she paused and then said that I was not as visible with her team as I could or should be. Wow! What a great thing for me to know and change. Hence, although PEER is specific to one employee and based on her own responses to certain survey questions, the true and immense value is in the engagement conversation between the manager and the employee. The unfortunate reality is that not enough of these engagement conversations are taking place. I smile and still shake my head at the palpable irony that her PEER report resulted in *me* needing to make a change, not her. I am taking the quality data services team to lunch next week.

DEVELOPING AND ACTING ON ENGAGEMENT GOALS

After discussing an employee's personal engagement level and determining any areas for improvement, the manager and employee should work together to come up with a list of goals to help improve the employee's engagement level. This list can include goals for both the employee and manager to achieve. If the employee took PEER, the suggestions given in the report can be used as a jumping-off point for this list of goals.

Once a list of goals has been determined, the manager and employee should set a time line for reaching each goal. By setting deadlines and checkpoints, the manager is ensuring that both parties are working to reach these goals. In addition, accountability is added into the process. The manager can then plan regular meetings to check in on any progress made toward achieving higher engagement levels.

MAINTAINING PERSONAL RESPONSIBILITY

One brilliant best practice to make sure employees stay on top of their personal engagement level is to encourage remote employees to self-motivate through daily or weekly reflective affirmations. These affirmations can include asking oneself:

- What did I enjoy most about my workday yesterday?
- How could I have done better?
- What did I learn this week in my job? What do I want to learn in the next week?
- Have I set clear and meaningful goals for myself to accomplish in the next month?
- When was the last time I challenged myself to get out of the comfort zone of doing the same job content by developing leading-edge and truly innovative work, crisply and cleanly letting go of the "time to make the donuts" mentality and approach to my job?
- Have I done a good job balancing my work life with my personal and family life, not forgetting, ignoring, or taking for granted the people and relationships I love the most?
- Have I been up-front and proactive in speaking with my manager about my engagement level?
- Have I taken control of my own engagement instead of falling into the trap of victimhood and persistent complaining and whining?
- Have I deliberately steered clear of the known troublemakers and gossip-mongers on the team, knowing they will drag me down?
- Have I let go of the things that make me irritable or grumpy, trying my best to let go and move on?
- Did I have fun while working yesterday?
- Did I do a great job this week by being supportive of my coworkers and contributing to the success of team and company goals?
- Did I do my absolute best to be engaged in my job yesterday?

- Did I call my manager and/or team members to discuss challenges and brainstorm ideas?
- Did I speak up during team meeting conference calls to offer my opinions and ask questions?

These reflections are valuable and inspirational to any employee, whether manager or non-manager, on-site or virtual. With that said, they are especially valuable to closing the gap of connectivity for virtual workers. In essence—and somewhat comically—the reflections create and nurture the remote employee's "friends" of Me, Myself, and I.

Employees who truly care about their personal level of engagement will carefully consider each question and determine how to improve questions that had negative answers.

A DIALOGUE WITH THE DISENGAGED

As you may have guessed, not all employees will be open to building a two-way relationship regarding their personal engagement. This issue is most common among actively disengaged employees, who don't especially care about their work or the outcomes they produce. Actively disengaged employees are particularly dangerous in virtual workplaces, where managers cannot keep tabs on any damaging behaviors they may exhibit. Simply put, virtual managers are not in as good of a position to detect smear campaigns, bad-mouthing, or gossip-mongering.

Despite the fact that disengaged employees don't usually want to have a discussion about their engagement (or lack thereof), it is still important to try to discuss what is holding them back from being engaged or even ambivalent. Understanding exactly why virtual employees are disengaged is fundamental, as virtual managers may not always be able to observe what is happening in various locations. Their reaction to the discussion (or simply the invitation to have such a discussion) can tell you a lot about their future with the company. If, during the discussion, the employee is able to come up with reasons why he or she is disengaged, as well as talk about potential ways to mitigate these issues, then the employee has the chance to one day rise out of the ranks of the disengaged.

However, if the employee is not open to the dialogue at all and offers no suggestions to improve his level of engagement, then it may be better for both you and the employee to cut your losses and part ways.

Disengaged employees are a cancer for a virtual team. Their negative attitudes and behaviors can infect those in contact with them, decreasing their coworkers' engagement levels. Ambivalent employees are especially susceptible, and placing them in close contact with disengaged employees can cause the disease of disengagement to quickly spread throughout an organization.

It makes sense that managers would want to do all they can to re-engage their employees. Terminating someone takes time and effort, and could lead to psychological stress; removing an employee from her position is damaging to managers and employees alike. In the remote world, it may be even more difficult, as managers need to examine the multiple communication channels and decide which is best to use. Arranging a time to terminate the individual or pick up equipment could be a lingering hesitation toward termination as well. However, the disengaged employees are an invariable lost cause, sapping and draining both time and resources, and managers may do well to transition these employees out of the workplace.

BUILDING HEALTHY RELATIONSHIPS

By taking responsibility for their engagement, remote employees are able to build healthy relationships with colleagues and reach the highest rungs on the corporate ladder, therefore succeeding in the virtual workplace. Distance employees and virtual managers alike will thus be climbing together toward organizational success.

Recognizing the contribution of every individual's unique engagement level, from management to entry-level, and how they interact, allows managers to develop methods and techniques for creating the most successful virtual workforce. Through this recognition, leaders can get the right people on the bus and driving in the right direction toward business success—an analogy made popular by Jim Collins, author of *Good to Great*. Exploring the 10 Key Drivers of Engagement (introduced in the next chapter) and tailoring them to your unique organization will allow you to create a virtual workforce every other organization will strive to emulate. Each subsequent chapter in this book will provide you with various and useful tools to achieve that goal.

CHAPTER 5

THE TOP 10 EMPLOYEE ENGAGEMENT DRIVERS: MAXIMIZING THEM FOR VIRTUAL WORKERS

Do you know what motivates your employees and influences their engagement? If you do not know why your virtual employees were attracted to the organization, their position, and the ability to work remotely, then simply ask. You might be surprised at the number of virtual managers who don't take the time to ask employees what drives them in the workplace. Consequently, these virtual managers have blindfolded themselves from a motivational management standpoint; they are befuddled as to why employee behaviors are not leading to the desired outcomes. These managers will continue to focus on the wrong issues, guessing about what may motivate and engage their employees. This guesswork causes employees to become frustrated and begin to head down the path of disengagement.

Round and round they go until someone finally notices that this system is not working and calls for some type of intervention. Do yourself a favor and do not get on the merry-go-round of motivational misalignment.

Instead of relying on guesswork, great virtual managers ask their employees about what really motivates them, as well as what might make them perform at a much higher and more engaged level. After asking each team member, the manager should make a list of the team's motivators. If there are major commonalities among the group (and there most frequently are), the virtual manager can use those shared drivers to design a motivation and engagement program for the team.

From decades of talent management research and analyses of millions of employee survey responses, HR Solutions' Research Institute has identified the Top 10 Key Drivers of Employee Engagement for virtual employees. These key drivers were found to have the greatest impact on employee engagement levels. The key drivers, in order of importance, are:

1. Recognition.
2. Career Development.
3. Direct Supervisor/Manager Leadership Abilities.
4. Strategy and Mission (especially the freedom and autonomy to succeed and contribute to the organization's success).
5. Job Content (the ability to do what I do best).
6. Senior Management's Relationship With Employees.
7. Open and Effective Communication.
8. Coworker Satisfaction/Cooperation (the unsung hero of retention).
9. Availability of Resources to Perform the Job Effectively.
10. Organizational Culture and Core/Shared Values.

By focusing on these areas, remote managers can make an enormous impact on their employees' engagement levels. In this chapter, I will discuss each key driver individually and share best practices to maximize employee engagement in a virtual team.

1. RECOGNITION

How often do you recognize your employees? Twenty years ago, you might have said just once a year. Annual recognition programs are now a thing of the past. Today, employees want and need to be recognized on a daily basis to stay engaged and productive in the workplace.

Many managers view recognition as an "extra," an initiative their employees like, but that isn't completely necessary. They could not be more wrong. HR Solutions' Research Institute has found that recognition has the largest impact on whether an employee is engaged. In fact, an employee's perception of recognition accounts for 56 percent of the variance of employee engagement.

Recognizing virtual employees is much more of a challenge than recognizing employees you see on a day-to-day basis. There simply aren't as many chances to slip in a quick thank you throughout the day. Unfortunately, remote managers actually tend to provide less recognition to their employees, when really they should be giving more. The more distanced employees are from their managers, the more recognition they need in order to stay effective. Remote managers must put in extra effort to give employees a virtual pat on the back and let them know their hard work is appreciated.

Remembering to recognize virtual employees on a regular basis can be tough for some managers. In order to provide the recognition virtual employees crave, managers should set daily, weekly, and monthly reminders to consider their employees' accomplishments and determine the correct means to recognize them. Although the methods of communication for recognizing virtual employees may be different, managers can still use the same types of recognition as they do with traditional employees.

Formal vs. Informal Recognition

The key to recognizing employees effectively is to utilize a mixture of formal and informal recognition. Formal recognition consists of recurring programs that recognize specific employees for specific accomplishments, and can include typical initiatives like employee-of-the-month programs. For virtual employees, this type of award should be given via video chat or conference call with an entire team, as it is meant to publicly and formally recognize the recipient. Formal recognition programs are a way of thanking employees for their high performance, and have a huge impact on the engagement level of recipients.

There is an issue with relying entirely on formal recognition programs, however: Built into the idea of formal recognition programs is the concept that recognition should only be given to the top performer, but top performers are not the only employees who should be recognized. It is also important for middle performers to receive recognition for their work, as positive feedback can often improve their performance. Informal recognition should be used to bridge the gap.

Informal recognition consists of any thanks or praise given to employees outside of formal recognition programs. For virtual employees, many managers take the easy road out and rely on electronic communication to recognize employees. Sending a quick thank-you via e-mail will help employees feel recognized, but it is not enough. According to research from Maritz, a consulting firm specializing in rewards and recognition, managers of remote employees must utilize several different methods and messages to truly maximize this driver of employee engagement.

A great way to mix things up is to send a hand-written thank-you note to the employee's home or work space. A personal card that you took the time to sit down and write shows employees that you really care about them and are sincere in your thanks and praise. In addition, it is something physical they can hold on to and show others, which will continue to remind them of your praise long after the note was written.

Picking up the phone and recognizing employees live is also a great way to boost this driver of engagement. A phone call (or video chat, if available) allows you to really convey your thanks and use tone and emotion to show sincerity. If the employee doesn't answer the phone, a voicemail can also do the trick.

To show appreciation for a large accomplishment, sending a gift to the employee is a great way to say thanks. A best practice is to send something that will brighten up the employee's work space, such as flowers or a plant. Another best practice is to send a gift card. The card should either be a general card that can be spent anywhere, such as American Express, or personalized to the employee's tastes and interests, such as a Starbucks gift card for a coffee fanatic.

Monetary vs. Experiential Rewards

Beware the mystic lure of cash. It is not the motivator you may think.

Money never made a man happy yet, nor will it. The more a man has, the more he wants.

—Benjamin Franklin

Cash is cash, and frankly, it is rather bereft of emotion. Cash is best used when fulfilling the basic promise implicit in the employer/employee relationship: pay, rather than as a reward. The best rewards are actually experiential, as these elicit an emotional response from employees. You can test this premise for yourself firsthand: Gauge the reaction you get when giving an employee a sterile $100 bill or direct deposit versus the response you get when rewarding an employee with a chance to win a vacation to Hawaii. Cash rewards have little recognition mojo because they are easily lost in the sea of expenses, checkbook entries, and the clutter of daily life. Emotions are powerful, and mightily influence behavior—skilled virtual managers harness them and ride them to the finish line.

Furthermore, cash-based reward systems create a calculative mindset, which create natural (and negative) questions in the employees' minds, such as:

- "That's all?"
- "I wonder how much Mary got...."
- "How much will I get next time?"

Other non-cash recognition rewards that elicit emotion are far more motivational. Non-cash recognition such as gift cards and gold clubs spur emotional appreciation as well as imagining experience. For example, these rewards spur thoughts of where the gift card can be tendered or what golf resort or hole at which you will first use that golf club.

Lastly, the emotional appeal of non-cash rewards, such as vacations, golf clubs, or even gift cards, spurs the employee recipient to talk about them. Have you ever heard an employee bragging about the $100 direct deposit that was put in his checking account? Of course not. Have you ever heard an employee bragging about the rewards-based vacation or brand-new Big Bertha golf club she won? Absolutely—and probably quite passionately at that.

In addition, many Best-in-Class employers and virtual managers rely on points-accumulation, non-cash reward and recognition systems to motivate employees. In these programs, employees earn points as they achieve performance goals. These points can later be turned in to receive a reward. Configuring non-cash recognition programs as accumulation on points-based systems unleashes the employees' emotions about **challenging themselves**, **achieving**, and **making progress**; these three feelings are major stimulants of employee engagement and business outcomes. The nature of accumulating and accruing rewards or points makes it a journey, as opposed to a one-time event.

Private vs. Public Recognition

Formal recognition programs should usually be conducted in public, such as during a staff meeting. However, informal recognition can be given at any time. This allows managers to provide informal recognition both publicly and privately.

Choosing whether to recognize an employee privately or publicly depends largely on the employee's needs. Some employees may be embarrassed by public recognition, whereas others may want their peers to know of their accomplishments. I make a point to always ask employees which type of recognition they prefer, and then cater to their preference. If possible, ask employees during the hiring process or during their first day on the job which type of recognition they prefer so that you can begin recognizing new employees from day one.

The challenge of providing informal recognition publicly for virtual employees is finding the correct time to do so. Managers can designate a chunk of time during staff or department meetings to recognize employees, or have employees thank one another. In addition, during meetings, virtual managers can detail who completed which parts of each project and compliment their work. By doing so, managers also open up the floor for others to recognize these employees.

Peer-to-Peer Recognition

Peer-to-peer recognition often happens in an informal manner among traditional employees, where employees thank and recognize each other in passing. For virtual employees, this type of recognition rarely takes place. It is important for managers to give employees a place to recognize one another, such as a virtual "thanks board." The thanks board (or "Snaps Board," as we call it in my office) is a place for employees to spontaneously praise and recognize their coworkers. This type of public recognition helps to create a sense of community among employees, which is especially important for virtual employees who never see their coworkers in person.

In addition, an organization can create a symbolic award that is passed from employee to employee to recognize excellence. At my company, our employees pass around the HR Solutions Apple. Every month, the Apple is passed to an employee who is living the company mission, going the extra mile, and exhibiting the behaviors of engagement. The passing of the Apple is done at all-staff meetings so everyone gets a chance to publicly recognize the recipient. For virtual employees, the symbolic award could be represented by a special stamp inserted into the recipient's e-mail signature, or it could be a physical award that is shipped from employee to employee. This type of recognition is great for virtual employees because they may not think to thank their coworkers without a formal program in place.

The double benefit of virtual peer-to-peer recognition programs is that it not only benefits recognition, but coworker satisfaction as well, another key driver of employee engagement. Coworker satisfaction can be trickier to build in virtual offices, where employees have little contact with one another. Having peer-to-peer recognition programs encourages employees to get to know one another and builds a sense of camaraderie among teammates. Coworker satisfaction is discussed in more detail later in this chapter.

2. CAREER DEVELOPMENT

The importance of career development is much more pronounced among virtual employees than any other group. There is an immense concern among remote workers that they will not be considered for promotions and will be passed up in favor of employees who work in the office. Their fear is a legitimate one. Remote employees have less face-time with "the powers that be" within their organizations, and therefore are less likely to come to mind as viable candidates. In addition, sometimes there is a perception that remote employees, especially those who work from home, are less serious about their careers. This fear of being passed up can be detrimental, as employees who believe they cannot advance within a company will look for advancement elsewhere. The point of many virtual programs is not only to allow additional workplace flexibility, but also to allow organizations to employ the best people regardless of their location. By not providing career development opportunities, organizations are essentially negating one of the most important benefits of virtual work. Virtual managers should take steps to make sure employees feel they receive enough attention and training to advance in their careers.

The best way to find out how employees feel about career development is to talk to them one-on-one. This type of conversation can be done over the phone, as most employees will be fairly candid about their desires and expectations. For employees who come into the office monthly or even quarterly, this conversation can be even more fruitful if conducted in person. Contrary to popular belief, conversations about career development do not need to coincide with formal performance evaluations. In fact, these types of conversations generally need to occur more frequently than performance evaluations in order to ensure employees stay on track to meet their career development goals.

Before having career discussions with employees, it is important for virtual managers to take a look at their organization's structure and determine which positions would be suited for virtual work. The fact that employees believe they are not eligible for senior positions because they work remotely can also be a root cause of career development concerns for virtual employees. Obviously not all positions are conducive to virtual work, but one should not take senior positions out of the running simply because they are senior positions. Many organizations employ senior leadership members who work remotely part or all of the time; this is especially true for sales positions. Certain leaders may have to travel more than other remote employees to be present at important meetings and events, but it is generally possible to allow them to work virtually. In fact, the nature of many senior positions is virtual, as these employees are often out of the office traveling to different company locations and meeting with clients. The trick is to determine a system to allow virtual leaders to meet all of their responsibilities.

During an employee's career development conversation, it's best to first get an idea of the employee's thoughts about his future within the organization. Next, the manager can lay out potential paths and offer the ability to travel these paths virtually, or to shift back and forth between virtual and non-virtual positions. A best practice is for managers to literally draw out career path opportunities so employees can map out a route for their career. To go along with a career map, there should be a corresponding training and development map to show employees the goals they must reach to facilitate career advancement. Assuring employees that they will be able to meet their career goals within the company while working virtually is extremely important, as it will alleviate any negative thoughts they may have about career advancement. It is also important to discuss whether certain paths would require the employee to work in the office rather than remotely, and to gauge the employee's interest in non-remote work.

The final part of career development discussions should focus on how the employee can reach her desired career goals. Is it through increased training? Taking on new responsibilities? Entering into a mentorship program? The manager and employee should iron out a clear plan as well as schedule future meetings to discuss the employee's progress. A best practice is for managers to meet quarterly with their employees to assess progress on their career plans, get feedback, and recalibrate if necessary.

Managers must show employees that they truly support employees' career goals. To do so, managers should account for training and development within their department budget. In addition, managers should provide their employees with the necessary time for training during working hours to allow employees the means to advance.

Training programs and mentorships are a great way to help employees reach their goals. Training can mainly be conducted virtually, but in-person training events are effective as well, and are a great way to get remote employees into the office now and then. (Training is discussed in more depth in Chapter 7.) Virtual mentorships, on the other hand, can be done remotely. A best practice is to assign mentors to remote workers who have been in their shoes—in other words, have worked remotely for at least part of their career—and have made significant advancements in their career throughout their tenure with the organization. These mentors will be able to give a different perspective on career advancement than those who have never worked remotely, as well as show that virtual career advancement is possible to achieve.

Because virtual work has become more popular recently, an organization may not have past virtual employees to act as mentors. In these cases, it may be possible for employees to find mentors from local professional networks. If this isn't an option, non-virtual employees from within the organization can act as mentors. However, in this case, employees should also be provided with success stories of other remote workers in their industry to provide inspiration.

To help employees believe that they can advance within their organization, it is also important for senior leaders to take the initiative to get to know and bond with virtual employees. Because senior leaders will not be bumping into these employees in the elevator or at the water cooler, they need to make a point to form professional relationships with them in order to even the playing field. Informal mentorships are a great way for senior leaders to not only get to know these employees, but also to develop future talent for the company. Creating formal and informal mentorships between senior leaders and virtual employees will not only help to maximize career development as a driver of employee engagement, but will also build a foundation to strengthen the organization as a whole.

3. DIRECT SUPERVISOR/MANAGER LEADERSHIP ABILITIES

There's a famous (but slightly outdated) proverb that says, "Behind every great man stands a great woman." In the workplace, that phrase can be revised to say, "Behind every great employee stands a great manager." Although it is possible to have highly engaged employees with mediocre managers, the majority of high performers are backed up by an excellent supervisor. Great managers support their employees and create an environment where they are more likely to succeed. In the virtual environment, the need for excellent managers is magnified because there is less face-to-face interaction with direct reports. Ultimately, virtual managers must work harder to foster excellent communication and build trust than managers who work on-site with their direct reports.

The direct supervisor/manager's leadership ability is one of the most important drivers of engagement, because the manager affects a number of other key drivers. Think about it—who directly recognizes employees? The manager. Who helps develop, foster, and nurture employees' careers? The manager.

Remarkable virtual managers possess all of the qualities outlined in Chapter 2, many of which focus on both building trust and erasing the feelings of isolation and lack of connectedness; hence, the following traits should be non-negotiable when hiring for virtual managers. They should be:

- Trustworthy and fantastic trust builders.
- Very able communicators.

- Talented team collaborators.
- Master architects with designing the virtual team's clear roles, responsibilities, and purpose.
- Experts at alignment with corporate strategy and mission.
- Stupendous, deliberate, and careful motivators.

As previously implied, it takes a special breed of manager to be able to supervise virtual employees, trusting they are actually working and that these employees will complete projects on time without continuous input and check-ins from the manager. Micromanaging absolutely does not work on a virtual level. Managers are not able to pop in and check that something is being completed or steer employees back on the right track. There has to be trust on the part of the manager that the employee understands assigned projects, has the information he needs to work on the projects, and will complete them on time.

That being said, managers cannot just throw projects into the wind and hope the employee catches them. Whereas micromanaging them will not work, providing guidance will. Guidance includes answering any questions employees may have, providing necessary materials and resources, and connecting employees with the right people and departments. Doing so will help employees to be more productive while still feeling independent.

Virtual managers must have exceptional guidance, organizational, and coordination skills in order to track what is being worked on by whom and when it will be completed. Otherwise, it is extremely easy for work to get lost in a virtual black hole. A best practice is to schedule a weekly meeting to talk with employees one-on-one regarding their project list and ensure nothing slips through the cracks. Remote managers should ask for feedback from employees as to whether these status meetings are occurring at the correct frequency to make sure employees get the attention they deserve, but do not feel as though they are being constantly monitored. Clearly, virtual managers must walk a fine line between over- and under-managing their employees.

Virtual managers must also have excellent interpersonal skills to succeed. When communicating with virtual employees over the phone or via e-mail, it is often hard to get a sense of how they really feel about a situation. Only 7 percent of the total impact of a message actually comes from the words used; 38 percent comes from tone and 55 percent is nonverbal.[1] When a person communicates via telephone, he or she only receives 45 percent of the message, and e-mail recipients miss more than 90 percent! A great option for managers is to video chat whenever possible with their employees. However, as video chatting is not always an option, successful virtual managers must have a keen ability to read people, or rather, to pick up on what isn't being said. They should have enough "virtual sensitivity" to discern when an employee is unhappy or confused. In addition, they should be able to make employees feel comfortable and reassure them without visual and sound-based cues.

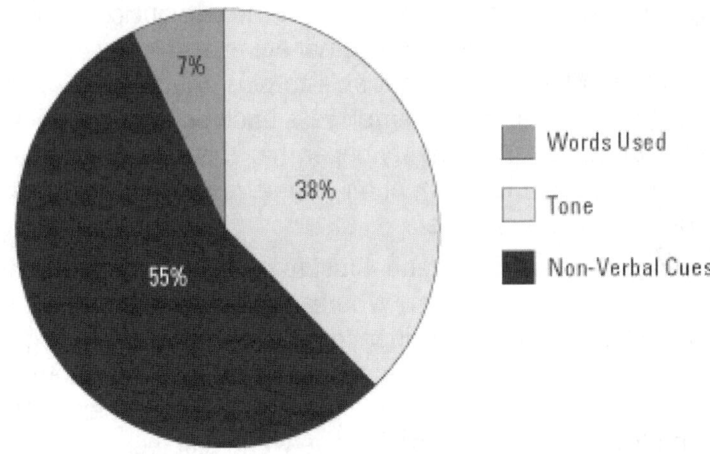

Message Interpretation

4. STRATEGY AND MISSION (ESPECIALLY THE FREEDOM AND AUTONOMY TO SUCCEED AND CONTRIBUTE TO THE ORGANIZATION'S SUCCESS)

As clearly outlined in Chapter 2, the need to establish clear meaning and purpose for the virtual worker cannot be overstated. Indeed, satiating the longing for connection of virtual workers by bonding them emotionally and intellectually to the organization's purpose is a definite best practice of the most outstanding virtual managers. Making it possible for employees to contribute to the organization's success is a key part of engagement.

Every human being wants to have a purpose. People have a natural desire to perform actions that lead to a desired net outcome. Their goals, whether work-related or personal, can be both grand and basic. Nonetheless, achieving these goals is especially important to each person.

In other words, as we go through life, we yearn to find *meaning* for the things we do.

There is no doubt that reaching or exceeding our goals is not easy. In fact, nearly all of these goals require some "heavy lifting," such as extra effort or careful thought, yet we try to do them gladly because we want to *achieve*. Thus, our goals quite naturally shape our actions. Although desired outcomes differ greatly from employee to employee, it is easy to conclude that, most of the time, people do not like to do things for no reason. If we cannot find *meaning* in what occupies our time, we are likely to stop doing it. Thus, *clarity of purpose* is a strong driver of engagement for any worker.

It is no different in the virtual workplace. In fact, when virtual employees are given an assignment, oftentimes they are not told why the task is of value to the organization; they are simply told to do the task. Hence, without any knowledge of how the task has meaningful purpose, they will be much less likely to want to do it, or they will wind up doing it "half-assed," as my father used to say. In addition, the virtual worker will probably not devote as much effort or careful attention to the project because she simply does not see or understand it as being important. This actuality is why it is paramount for managers to communicate the importance of each and every role within an organization, and the job functions related with that role.

Intelligent virtual managers will leverage the strategy and mission driver to the maximum. They can do so by taking the time to articulate the meaning and purpose of their virtual employees' tasks and jobs. Certain jobs lend themselves very nicely to this dialogue. For instance, it is pretty easy to put into words the meaningfulness and value of being a firefighter, police officer, nurse, or doctor: "You save lives and keep people safe from harm!" Teachers are another no-brainer. What person would claim teaching had little or no credible purpose?

But what about people who are call center operators, envelope stuffers, data entry staff, mail sorters, assembly line workers with the same repetitive motion in their job, and janitors? How does the virtual manager successfully imbue the meaningfulness of these jobs? Lawyers? Give that one a go and you'll find yourself thinking it is easy to express the meaningful purpose half the time, and the other half of the time, you might be laughing or shaking your head. The reality is that successfully putting into words the significance and importance of any job is relatively easy, **as long as the manager gives it some careful thought up-front**.

Let's take a close look at the janitorial services position. The function requires cleaning filth, eradicating "accidents" and messes (created by someone else), and tidying up toilets and urinals. In the virtual environment, employees who clean Porta-Pottys or those who pick up road kill have similar engagement challenges. What chance do you have of engaging employees by convincing them of how meaningful and critically important their job is to their coworkers, the organization, and society at large? Actually, a very good chance, if you are a smart and caring manager.

For instance, caring managers will take the time to craft a real truth about how one particular job helps others. In the case of our janitorial Services workers, the manager can take the time to explain to all employees that their work creates a clean environment, which in turn keeps other people healthy. In the case of the environmental services worker at a hospital, the manager can share the wonderful certainty that the employees' work actually saves lives. Few people know it, but the Center for Disease Control and Prevention estimates that 1.7 million hospital-acquired infections occur each year, leading to approximately 99,000 deaths in the United States alone. Shockingly, research shows that an individual is five times more likely to die from seeking medical care than to be killed in a homicide. This department-specific example is near and dear to my heart largely because many other workers wrongfully look down on or ignore these very special people who work in environmental services, when in fact they should be admiring both them and their work.

In any given year, I physically visit roughly 50 different hospitals, largely due to HR Solutions' strong practice in the healthcare vertical. Based upon my experience, I estimate that a mere 15 percent of environmental services department directors have positioned the importance of the work, as I have described. If you by chance were one of these janitorial workers, would you feel as though you were really even a part of the organization, let alone connected to its overall strategy and mission? Most likely, you would not. Frankly, I find that sad. I do not believe this lack of management communication is done maliciously, but rather that the manager has simply not taken the time to craft the candid and straightforward story on the job function's importance and meaningfulness. HR Solutions' survey statistics also point out that this is a pretty common talent management challenge, as we have found that most organizations' environmental services department employees have considerably more unfavorable perceptions of this strategy and mission–related key driver than other departments.

I am utterly convinced that with some careful and caring thought on the part of the manager, even the most boring jobs can be positioned as important and meaningful. If you Google "Most Boring Jobs" on the Web, you will likely find envelope stuffers, mail sorters, data entry personnel, and some industry-specific security guards. You might even run into a video I watched that visually documented the mail sorter job. While viewing it, I surmised that I would rather watch paint dry than do that job; I was literally yawning within ten seconds of watching the video footage.

I then shared the search results with my wife, who told me about one of her first jobs in high school at an area office-products supplier. She and a fellow coworker were tasked with sharing the exciting job of sitting in a dank room near the employee entrance at the back of building, monitoring and greeting those who entered and exited. Because they worked alone, with infrequent visits from employees arriving at work, "management" gave them the all-important task of removing staples from paper documents so the "extremely sensitive" documents could be shredded; the reality is that most of the documents were not extremely sensitive and the staples could probably have been much more efficiently removed by a machine. Making matters even worse, she was not allowed to leave her work station without pre-approval, even for a brief visit to the bathroom. That workplace regulation conjures up images of having to raise your hand back in second grade in order to use the facilities. Needless to say, she and her friend did not feel stapled to the strategic importance of their job, but rather stapled on a meaningless and needless job. I suspect she and her coworker developed an early and strong lifelong friendship through the "misery loves company" reality, staple by staple.

As my wife shared this experience with me, my 9-year-old daughter Hannah asked if she could be interviewed for "the book." I said, "Sure. What is the most boring and meaningless job you ever had?" She retorted, "Making my bed and cleaning my room." When I asked why, it became abundantly clear that her reasoning was very much akin to the sentiments of most workers, virtual or not: "It is just not fun. I would rather be spending my time doing fun stuff." Sage advice from a 9-year-old that hits upon a proven best practice of employee engagement: Make a concerted effort to build fun into the workplace, and engagement will follow.

Finally, only 64 percent of employees feel that other staff members at their organization understand the strategy and mission.[2] Considering that the desire to contribute to the organization's goals is a top engagement driver, it is imperative that employees have a better understanding of the strategy and mission. When the overall strategy and mission are clearly defined, employees can more easily align themselves with the organization's ideals, mission, and success strategies. Our work in surveying millions of people about how they feel about a variety of strategy and mission–related subjects has yielded one seminal and key discovery: Communicating the stated and defined strategy and mission is the easy part; getting employees to breathe, live, and become passionate about intertwining the strategy and mission is the most daunting, poignant, and difficult challenge. As a participant in one of the focus groups I personally conducted for a client exclaimed, "Enough of the Wall Candy" (strategy, mission, and values posters). "I get it. I get it. I get it. You've drilled it into my brain and even put it on the back of my employee ID. You made me memorize it. But no one has told me how my job fits into the picture. I have no idea how my job contributes to the organization's success with the strategy and mission."

As previously implied, employees feel pretty comfortable with their organization's stated strategy and mission ("I agree with strategy": 74 percent favorable). To me, the most illuminating take-away from this data is the employees' rather tepid satisfaction with senior leaders demonstrating and communicating how their actions align with said strategy ("Senior leader's actions align with strategy": 63 percent; "Senior leader's actions are consistent with communication": 54 percent). The bottom-line message for all senior leaders is: Make sure you walk the talk. Refer to the chart on page 115 for more information.

Managing vs. Coaching

A lot of managers think their job duties match exactly to their title—managing. Virtual managers generally do well enough when it comes to responding to issues, managing day-to-day operations within their team, and coordinating projects. However, for remote managers, simply managing employees is not enough to build a strong working relationship and create a culture of high engagement and high performance.

Success or failure rests firmly on the way these managers approach their roles. Truly great managers don't just manage; they also coach their employees. Coaches are true leaders, and excellent coaches can adeptly transform a good team into a great team. Coaches are an inspiration for their team, providing vision and innovation to help elevate the team and its performance to whole new levels. Coaches also develop meaningful

Survey Items Related to Strategy and Mission

Best-in-Class Norm*	Norm (1% Favorable)	Dimension or Item
82	**66**	**Strategy/Mission Dimension**
87	74	I agree with the organization's strategy and mission.
82	69	The organization makes it possible for employees to diectly contribute to its success.
81	66	This organization has realistic goals and objectives.
82	66	This organization has a clear sense of direction.
80	65	Employees who work here understand the organization's strategy and mission.
	84	**Mission/Alignment/Balanced Scorecard Items**
82	74	My supervisor's actions are consistent with the organization's strategy and mission.
85	73	I can explain the organization's strategy/mission to my family, friends, and coworkers.
89	73	I am confident about this organization's future.
72	72	This organization's mission/strategy makes me feel that my job effort here is important.
80	63	Senior management's actions are in alignment with the organization's strategy and mission.
67	54	Senior management's actions are consistent with what they communicate.

**Best-in-Class: 90th percentile score.*

The Correlation Coefficient (r) is a value that quantifies the relationship between two variables. The value of r can be between +1.00 (positive correlation) and -1.00 (negative correlation). A positive correlation signifies that one variable becomes larger as the other variable becomes larger (i.e., height vs. weight); therefore, a perfect correlation would yield a score of +1.00. A negative correlation, or inverse relationship, shows that as one variable becomes larger the other becomes smaller (i.e., weight vs. gymnastic ability); a perfect negative correlation would be -1.00. The absolute lack of a correlation, meaning there is no relationship between two variables, would yield a score of 0. A score of .71, as shown in the chart above, is considered a strong correlation. Correlations do not imply causation, but rather show a relationship.

relationships with their employees that help to show they care about the employee and make every effort to enhance his or her personal job engagement. These special coaches know that putting the "human" back in human capital management yields enormous dividends. Thus, in order to truly maximize this driver of engagement, virtual managers must care, coach, and coordinate—the ultimate triumvirate for management success.

Despite the distance, it is still possible for remote managers to perform impeccably on all three of the success traits for coaches. One important aptitude for great virtual managers is the ability to achieve a balance between being seen as an authority and as an actual person who puts his or her pants on the very same way as the virtual employee. Remote employees need to see that there is someone at the mast of the ship. Standing your ground shows employees that you are in charge and are leading the team to greatness.

However, true leaders also show concern for their employees and care about them as people. Thus, talented virtual managers will also recognize the instances regarding standards and deadlines that warrant special exception. A best practice for virtual managers is to take the time to ask about employees' lives both inside and outside of their work life whenever possible. When the majority of communication is conducted via e-mail, small talk is usually completely cut out of the conversation. Small talk and chit-chat may seem unproductive, but they are vital to building strong relationships with employees. Taking the time to truly relate to virtual employees will help to build their engagement levels.

5. JOB CONTENT (THE ABILITY TO DO WHAT I DO BEST)

Children decide what they want to be when they grow up based on their impression of job content. Naturally, we all want to be *passionate* about our career because it is such a major part of adult life, and job content is where most people focus first. For example, a child might want to be a marine biologist because he likes dolphins and wants to swim with them. Another child might want to be a pilot because she thinks flying fighter jets is cool. As we grow up, we realize job content is generally much more complex than simply completing one task day in and day out. Marine biologists might spend a portion of their workday in the water with dolphins, but certainly not all day every day, and fighter pilots actually spend much more of their time on land than in the air. In addition, both positions undoubtedly involve less glamorous assignments, such as completing some type of paperwork as well as other menial tasks. As adults, we understand that in order to do something we love, we will most likely also have to spend time working on aspects that are less exciting.

If you are like most people, certain facets of your job remind you of exactly why you chose your career path, and others undoubtedly make you want to take a nap. Does that mean you are in the wrong position? Certainly not. All jobs have their ups and downs when it comes to required tasks: this balance between these tasks affects perceptions of job content, and plays a part in employee engagement. In fact, job content is the fifth-most-influential engagement driver, and likely more complex than you might have realized.

Managers often erroneously assume there are limited opportunities for increasing employee engagement through job content because certain tasks simply have to be completed. With this mindset, managers overlook simple adjustments that would actually make a big impact on engagement. For example, although it might not be possible to eliminate or alter certain tasks and assignments, there is likely some flexibility in *who* works on the assignment or *how* they work on it. Accommodating individuals' preferences for job content is best done as a team. If one employee dislikes a certain task, perhaps a different employee happens to like that task and they could trade assignments. Managers should be proactively asking questions to facilitate any quick and easy adjustments that would impact engagement.

One way to ameliorate perceptions of job content is to educate employees on the purpose of various tasks. People want their work to be meaningful, as this provides a sense of purpose and strikes to the heart of engagement. Oftentimes, the tasks employees work on are an integral part of the success of the organization, but workers do not know how their assignments fit into the big picture. Virtual workers have increased difficulty in this regard because they cannot always see from a distance how and why their work is needed. Virtual managers must get in the habit of communicating the "why" behind assignments so that employees fully understand the value of their hard work. Employees should also be encouraged to let one another know how their colleagues' efforts have helped make their own assignments easier. A great time to do this is in virtual meetings by allowing employees to speak up and recognize their coworkers' efforts. Ensuring that employees understand how their job content makes a difference to others and the organization overall is essential for capitalizing on this engagement driver.

Job content relates to what people actually *do* during the workday, and, oftentimes (and more importantly), it relates to *how* they do it. The work environment plays a major factor in how people do their work, and it greatly contributes to giving employees the opportunity to do what they do best. It is surprising how underestimated the impact of employees' surroundings and physical location on their engagement can be by employers. In reality, many people choose their career path because of their desired work environment.

For example, some people cannot picture themselves being happy doing *any* type of work if it required sitting in a cubicle day in and day out. For others, working alone in a home office and rarely seeing coworkers in person does not seem remotely appealing, regardless of the project or assignment. These preferences for work environment are deeply ingrained in who we are on a personal level. When people work in a setting that isn't a good fit for their personality, it limits their ability to do what they do best, simply by the nature of their environment.

Some people do avoid certain industries or career paths because they know the work environment wouldn't be a great fit, but others do not. Even if a person does not particularly enjoy working in a traditional office setting, it might go hand-in-hand with the type of work he enjoys most. This creates a dissonance in feelings related to the job, and thus engagement.

Think about it: When you are in an environment you don't like, it is very hard to enjoy what you are doing. For example, you are at the movie theater on a date with the person you care about. The movie is shaping up to be one of your all-time favorites, but you can't really hear it because there is a screaming baby next to you. It's also incredibly cold in the theater, and you just can't get comfortable. Additionally, the smell of cleaning fluid is overwhelming. Even though you're watching a great movie, are you enjoying yourself? Probably not. In fact, you would rather have gone to a different movie that wasn't as good, but provided a much better viewing experience.

Employees view job opportunities the same way. It isn't just *what* they do it's *how* (and *where*) they do it. Engaged employees are intrinsically motivated to do their best work. When people can control their work environment, they are able to create a work space that is conducive to their personal work style and engagement. A quiet, comfortable space with limited distractions is definitely a part of a good work environment, but it goes beyond that.

Many positions that are suitable for distance working are "knowledge positions," or those that require expertise in specific subject areas. Knowledge workers have a heightened need for concentration, as many of their tasks are based around deep thinking. According to Sandy Burud, PhD, principal at Flex Employment Services, professionals who hold these positions thrive on autonomy even more than employees in other job functions. Burud says knowledge workers are motivated first by the work itself and "the ability to do the work in the way they believe to be most effective," which can mean the option to work remotely.[3] In fact, 40 percent of knowledge workers work from home at least one day per week.[4] Burud credits Peter Drucker with pointing out that knowledge workers by definition understand how to do their job better than their manager. They therefore expect their managers to treat them as equals, rather than subordinates, and are particularly frustrated (and ineffective) in a "command and control" environment. Burud discovered the characteristics of knowledge workers as a visiting scholar at the Peter Drucker School of Management in preparing her book on managing human capital. She has seen them play out throughout her 25 years of organizational consulting. To maintain these employees' engagement levels, managers are most successful when they support an autonomous environment that makes distance working possible.

Although managers might have limited flexibility in changing the assignments employees receive, they can take a different approach to engagement by allowing employees the freedom to choose *how* they work on their assignments. Providing the option to work virtually is oftentimes enough to significantly impact perceptions of job content and bolster engagement.

6. SENIOR MANAGEMENT'S RELATIONSHIP WITH EMPLOYEES

An employee's relationship with senior management, whether the employee works remotely or not, is imperative to nurturing employee engagement. Strong relationships help increase the level of trust that employees have in their leaders. Increased trust helps to get employee buy-in for new ideas, and also builds employee engagement. Due to distance, virtual employees rarely receive the same amount of face-time with senior management as employees who work on-site. This lack of visibility can cause remote workers to feel disconnected from senior leadership as well as from the organization itself. Unfortunately, CEOs and other C-suite employees are often unsure of how to overcome this barrier to engagement.

Building a strong relationship with their employees is not an impossible feat for senior leaders to achieve. Just ask Frits van Paasschen, president and chief executive officer of Starwood Hotels & Resorts Worldwide. Starwood Hotels has just more than one thousand employees located at their corporate headquarters in White Plains, New York, but more than 200,000 employees at various locations across the globe. Rather than dropping the ball when it comes to visibility among his employees, van Paasschen made a conscious effort to pick up the ball and run with it. Every week, van Paasschen travels across the globe, stopping in at every Starwood location where he can in order to get in face-time with as many employees as possible. In the spring of 2011, he spent a month visiting locations in China. This type of visit is not so much for the benefit of himself, but rather for the benefit of Starwood's employees. With his constant travel schedule through multiple time zones, van Paasschen often ends up tired when his plane touches down in a new location. Before exiting the plane, however, he always takes the time to mentally pump himself up. "For many employees, this is the first or only time they'll ever see their CEO," said van Paasschen. "I have to make every visit count, and remember that it isn't about me. It's about the employees."[5]

Making Visits Valuable

When senior leaders like van Paasschen are able to make in-person visits to their employees, there are several best practices they can follow to make the visit as valuable as possible for remote employees. First, before arriving, senior leaders can ask for a list of the top performers within the location. The leader can then make a personal stop at each top performer's desk or invite the top performers to a group lunch. Top performers are likely to gain the most benefit out of meeting directly with senior leadership because they care the most about the organization.

Another best practice is for the senior leader to speak to all employees at the location about the organization's strategy and mission. Employees are likely to understand their connection to the strategy and mission if they are able to learn about it directly from senior leadership (organizational strategy and mission was discussed in more detail earlier in this chapter).

At larger organizations, it may only be possible for a visiting senior leader to speak with all employees at once, in a large-town-hall type meeting. However, at smaller organizations, a best practice is for the senior leader to meet with each department individually to speak to employees and discuss any concerns they may have. This individualized attention and interaction will have a greater impact on the visibility of senior management and help employees to feel a personal connection to the senior leader.

Adding a Personal Touch

For virtual employees working out of home offices, personal visits from the senior management team are probably not feasible. However, there are other ways for leadership to stay visible to virtual employees. One way is to host a video forum, in which employees are able to ask questions and make comments directly to the CEO or other senior leader, who can answer via video. Video forums are a great way for employees to personally interact with senior managers and see that the leaders of their organization are real, live people. Members of the senior leadership team can also create personal blogs, video blogs, or Twitter accounts to interact with employees.

When possible, a best practice is for senior leaders to reach out directly to employees regarding new initiatives to show the change is coming from the top. When communicating new initiatives with employees, senior managers should consider the voice in their message. Most messages from senior leadership tend to be carefully worded and edited, making the message seem scripted and impersonal. To help messages seem more sincere, they should try to cut down on jargon and corporate-speak. By removing this type of language, employees are more likely to feel the message is coming directly from that leader, and will feel as though a personal touch was added to the message.

Responding to Employees

After asking for feedback from employees, senior management must act on the information they receive. In an environment of "doing more with less" and ongoing change, the front-line employees are often the best sources of innovative and productive ideas; therefore, an organization can truly benefit from improving the upward flow of communication to management while incurring very little, if any, additional cost. If senior leadership is not willing to put the time or effort into responding to employee concerns, then it is better not to ask for feedback at all. Just as we advise our clients conducting employee surveys, to ask for feedback and do nothing in response is actually worse than not conducting the survey at all, as it hurts employee opinions and will put a damper on any future initiatives.

7. OPEN AND EFFECTIVE COMMUNICATION

"What's going on?" We often hear or think that phrase several times a day. Everyone wants to be in the know about the things affecting them on a daily basis, especially within the virtual workplace. In order to build any engaged workforce, there must be a strong focus on open and effective communication. If people do not know what is going on, they make assumptions, frequently leading to misperceptions about their employer and/or their manager.

With the expansion of both global offices and remote workers, communication is even more vital today than it was in years past. Without communication, it would not be possible for employees to be connected to their organization. Communication truly is the vehicle through which engagement exists.

HR Solutions' Research Institute has found a strong correlation between communication and overall job satisfaction/employee engagement in our Best-in-Class and Most Improved clients.[6]

A +0.71 is a strong positive correlation indicating that when communication scores are high, overall job satisfaction and engagement scores tend to be high. The inverse is also true: As senior management

The Top 10 Employee Engagement Drivers

communicates more openly and frequently with employees, employees become more engaged. Regular, effective communication between senior management and employees is essential for building both employee engagement and satisfaction.

Given communication's significant role in fostering a culture of engagement, it is important to evaluate how employees *currently receive* organizational information and how they *prefer to receive* said information. HR Solutions' research shows a misalignment occurring in the workplace as it relates to communication.

I currently receive most of this organization's information from:	*Meetings or discussions with my supervisor*	*My coworkers*	*The employee newsletter*	*Organization memos and/ or paycheck stuffers*	*E-mail/ Intranet*
NORM	35	26	6	7	24
I prefer to receive most of this organization's information from:	*Meetings or discussions with my supervisor*	*My coworkers*	*The employee newsletter*	*Organization memos and/ or paycheck stuffers*	*E-mail/ Intranet*
NORM	52	6	6	10	24

The data in the table on the previous page identifies a significant gap when considering where employees prefer to get their information and where they are actually receiving their information. There are two core things to take away from this research. First is the glaring discrepancy between how many people want to hear things from their manager and how many actually receive this direct communication. This gap is often created due to a common default reaction of managers to immediately go back to work following an announcement made during a management meeting. However, in this situation, to bridge the gap it would be much more effective for management to have a huddle or communication with their direct reports to share any news or events that affect them and their perception of the workplace.

The second point to take away from the research, which is even more alarming, is that the majority of employees report their number-one source for information as their "coworkers." This is particularly disturbing because this source is essentially the grapevine, and employees are relying upon hearsay as opposed to factual information they could be receiving though management.

If virtual workers are not kept informed, they may often assume the worst, filling in the blanks with assumptions, negativity, and incorrect conclusions. The old adage of "no news is good news" is completely false when managing the virtual worker.

Communicate, communicate, communicate. You will know when to stop when they ask you to do so. Changing your communication paradigm and assumptions is essential to maintaining a connection with virtual workers. It is vital to bridge the communication gap between the head office and the virtual workplace.

8. COWORKER SATISFACTION/ COOPERATION (THE UNSUNG HERO OF RETENTION)

Coworker satisfaction and cooperation is one of the most often overlooked drivers of employee engagement. Managers often see this driver as something out of their control and an issue not worth worrying about. After all, how are managers supposed to influence whether their employees get along, or enjoy working together?

Coworker relationships are extremely important in the workplace, as they have a strong influence on day-to-day satisfaction and engagement. In fact, coworker satisfaction and employee engagement have a Pearson Correlation of +0.45, which indicates a fairly strong positive correlation. (As mentioned earlier, a positive *correlation* means that as one variable increases, the other increases as well.) Thanks to this positive relationship, I have always referred to coworker satisfaction as "The Unsung Hero of Retention." Coworker relationships are the glue that binds employees to the organization; simply put, it makes it really tough for people to leave the organization for other employment. There are literally hundreds of millions of employees around the globe who feel they are underpaid and unappreciated, dislike their supervisors, can't relate to their organization's mission and values, and dislike their job duties, yet still come into work each day because they enjoy working with Mary or John. If an employee does not have strong coworker relationships or feels negatively about coworkers, then the employee is less likely to feel a strong connection to the organization and therefore more likely to look for a job elsewhere.

For the virtual manager, the cold, hard reality is that coworker satisfaction is one of the most difficult drivers of employee engagement on which to influence improvement. After all, how are employees supposed to build relationships with coworkers they rarely or never actually see? Think about it: There are no casual conversations in the hallways to learn about coworkers' families or personal lives; no spontaneous elevator conversations. Coworkers cannot share the drive to the office or make plans for the weekend. There are no inside jokes to share because employees only interact in a formal manner. Due to this issue, employees who work virtually are more likely to feel detached, distanced, apart, separated, far-flung, and isolated, which can cause dissatisfaction and disengagement. These employees, who may be working from their home offices, attics, or basements, can feel extremely lonely and have an insatiable hunger for acknowledgement. To build camaraderie among employees, managers should focus on the following areas:

- Team bonding.
- Small talk.
- Team collaboration.
- Job Buddies.

Team Bonding

Team-building activities may need to be altered slightly, but it is still possible to conduct these exercises among remote workers. For example, instead of physical activities such as "trust falls," in which employees fall backward into another person's arms to learn trust, groups can play name games via video chat or play team video games as a group. Team-building activities serve a number of purposes for virtual employees. First, as previously noted, they help to build trust, which is vital in a working relationship. These types of activities also allow employees to interact outside their normal working roles and get to know one another. Any type of activity in which employees are encouraged to reveal fun or interesting facts about themselves can help to build personal connections and increase team camaraderie. This type of interaction creates the foundation for successful virtual coworker relationships.

A best practice from HR Solutions and our Best-in-Class clients to encourage team bonding is through staff Fun Fact Cards. These cards include a picture, information about the employee's personal and work history, and fun facts about the employee. At HR Solutions, these cards are posted in the kitchen for everyone to see. For virtual employees, they could be put on the company intranet, so that each time an employee logs in they see a different coworker's Fun Fact Card. Alternatively, the cards could be used to create a screensaver for company computers, allowing employees to cycle through their coworkers' cards.

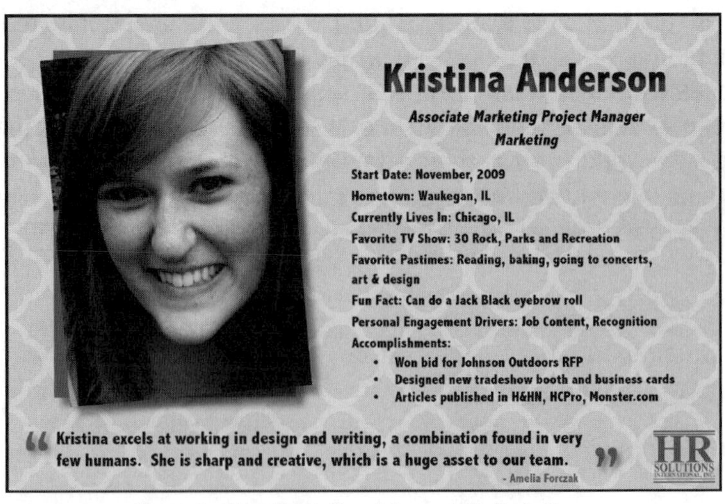

Sample Fun Fact Card from HR Solutions.

Another way to encourage team bonding is through company parties. These celebrations allow employees to let their hair down and get to know one another on a more personal level. For an annual party, if possible, the organization should pay for all employees to attend, even those who live quite far away. It really is not practical for employees to video chat at a party, as they will feel left out unless there is a specific ceremony or similar event they are viewing.

Company parties are also a great opportunity for employees to recognize each other by giving out departmental nicknames or staff superlatives, such as Tidiest Workspace or Best Laugh. These nicknames or superlatives can be silly, funny, or serious, but should come from employees' coworkers, not their managers or senior leaders. The point of giving each other nicknames or awards is for employees to really think about their coworkers' personalities, skills, and achievements, and recognize each other in a unique and fun way.

Small Talk

In an e-mail-heavy relationship, it is very easy to pass along work-related information. However, what's often missing from e-mail communication is a personal touch. Employees gain a lot from learning about their coworkers' personal lives, including a new perspective on employees' behaviors and attitude thanks to knowledge of their background and home life. However, people who e-mail are likely to jump straight past the small talk and get right down to business. In addition, people often use a formal tone in e-mails that they would not utilize when speaking to a coworker in person. Whereas professionalism is needed in the workplace, especially when communicating with clients and customers, it is not always necessary in exchanges between coworkers. E-mails can build a giant barrier between employees, impeding their ability to build relationships with each other.

As mentioned earlier in this chapter, managers should try to break away from the e-mail pattern when communicating with their employees. This rule should also apply to employees themselves when communicating with each other. Whenever possible, employees should opt to use video chat or the telephone to speak with one another. Instant messaging is also a good option for communication, as it is much more informal in nature and, as does the telephone, allows for back-and-forth interaction, which in turn allows for better collaboration on projects. In addition, employees get the chance to joke with one another and share details of their work and home lives. A good rule could be to dedicate the first five minutes of meetings to small talk and chatting. Coworkers can take turns giving personal updates or sharing fun facts about themselves. For large groups, one or two people could give an update at each meeting to ensure that small talk does not take over the meeting.

If possible, organizations should try to get remote workers together to meet and work with their team in person. An in-person meeting may seem expensive, but the benefits of in-person interaction simply cannot be equaled by any other type of communication. For remote workers living in close proximity, a weekly or monthly in-person meeting is a best practice. For employees who are geographically spread out, an annual meeting or company event is a great excuse to get coworkers together. In addition, distance coworkers could get together at trade shows, conferences, or training activities.

Team Collaboration

It is important to remember that just because employees may be working in different locations does not mean that they cannot work together and collaborate on projects. Virtual employees need to know that they are a part of a team. Being assigned collaborative projects will help them to feel that their coworkers support their efforts, which also improves trust. In addition, group projects encourage additional communication among team members, which is often lacking among remote teams.

Job Buddies

Remote workers may still feel out of the loop when it comes to interoffice news. A good remedy for this issue is to assign an on-site Job Buddy who is responsible for keeping her partner informed of what's going on at the office. The Job Buddy should be located at the organization's main branch or headquarters in order to be "in the know" about company news. The Job Buddy can be in charge of letting her partner know more about formal measures, such as new policies, as well as informal news, such as a coworker getting engaged. The Job Buddy is able to serve as a point person who can be contacted for any type of question the remote employee may have, and is able to help virtual employees feel connected to the organization.

9. AVAILABILITY OF RESOURCES TO PERFORM THE JOB EFFECTIVELY

Throughout the past 20-plus years of talent management consulting I've done, I've conducted more focus groups and analyzed more employee engagement survey data than I can count. I won't lie to you; there are moments when I'm meeting with teams of employees or examining survey responses and I think, "Wow. Now I've heard it all." Sometimes these moments result in cocktail-party stories—the woman who survived a heart attack at work but was written up for an unexcused absence from leaving work for the emergency room; the manager who purposefully made his direct reports look bad so he would appear more competent. Throughout the years I have collected so many stories, they have actually become fodder for one of my favorite speeches to present at national and international conferences: *Why Smart People Make Stupid Decisions*. Many times, the most jaw-dropping stories are a direct result of what I like to call "failing the stupid test" when it comes to the availability of resources to perform the job effectively.

On too many occasions, I have seen organizations tee their employees up for the perfect shot, only to turn around and hand them the wrong club. These organizations look great on paper; they have beautifully executed training, laudable career tracking, and award-winning employee recognition programs. Then I read survey results and learn employees are disengaged because they lack the necessary resources to perform their jobs effectively. For example, I've seen employees waste time cleaning the same floor twice due to poor-quality mops, or take an extra 30 minutes to transport a patient from X-ray due to an inadequate number of wheelchairs. Yes, my response is always the same: "Executive team, this is a no-brainer. Minimal cost, maximum impact. Purchase the mops. Increase the number of wheelchairs. It's time to pass the stupid test."

Determining the Resources Needed

If you've put time and energy into creating a magnetic culture, don't hinder your remote employees' ability to be productive by denying them access to necessary resources or by failing to create appropriate policies for tools and equipment. Just like your on-site employees, remote employees also require resources, tools, and technology to support their work, drive productivity, and facilitate real-time collaboration between employees and customers alike. As a virtual manager, it is in your best interests to ensure all employees have the resources they need to complete their job duties to the best of their ability. Whether that means having a printer/copier/fax machine in their home, or a GPS system in their car so they can easily navigate sales routes, as a general rule, allocating money to supplies and equipment pays dividends.

Although managers and employees often agree that certain supplies would be helpful in a virtual role, when it comes to who is responsible for purchasing and maintaining this equipment, there can be less of a consensus. Which supplies will your organization deem worthy of covering? Will you pay for expenses differently if employees work remotely full-time or part-time? It is essential to determine answers to these questions and develop a written policy before allowing employees to work virtually.

A great way to track proper resources for working remotely is to create a master list of the tools and resources employees need in various positions. Managers can create the lists, but employees should have the opportunity to make suggestions for additions, as they experience the virtual work environment firsthand. This list can be broken down into categories, such as "need to have" tools (i.e., Internet and phone) and "nice to have" resources (i.e., personal UPS/FedEx pickup or first-class upgrades for longer business flights). Employers should agree up front that virtual workers will be provided with all of the "need to have" items through direct purchase or fair compensation through reimbursement.

Regarding the "nice to have" list, employers should consider how these items could help employees be more productive or more engaged—thus, why these items could be worth the extra cost. Virtual managers should have a conversation with employees individually about their preference for tools and supplies, and try to help meet their needs. Managers can impact employee engagement in this regard simply by showing their concern for employees.

Expense Logistics

Some organizations find the easiest way to ensure remote employees have the resources they need is to provide them with a monthly expense stipend. For example, a company might choose to provide its virtual staff members with a $300 monthly stipend to cover general expenses such as office supplies (small ticket items), broadband connection expenses, and phone and data charges. With this arrangement, employees can meet their own needs by using the money as they see fit. Some organizations request that employees track and submit their purchase history, whereas others do not. Tracking expenses is great to gain a better understanding of actual costs, but it requires more time on behalf of the employer. If managers know employees' routine expenses are close to the stipend amount (ideally, slightly lower), going without expense reports demonstrates trust and saves time.

Alternately, if your organization would rather pay for exact expense amounts rather than monthly stipends, expense reports and receipts are a must, whether virtual employees have company credit cards or they get reimbursed. Once you have identified and defined what constitutes a business expense, it is critical to have a clear-cut policy for record-keeping expectations and approvals. You will save money by avoiding inconsistencies. Good practices include requiring managerial approval of any supplies and equipment expenses above a designated amount, and requiring employees to file an expense report within a certain time frame after the expense is incurred. Making the submission process quick and easy for virtual employees is important for productivity. Creating an online vehicle by which employees can upload receipts, import credit card statements, and complete expense reports for submission is recommended.

In summary, ensuring that virtual employees have a good understanding of the resources they need, and supporting them in obtaining these resources, is essential for engagement.

People as Resources

Sometimes we don't realize how much we learn from our colleagues just from being around them. When working in close proximity with co-workers, we oftentimes become familiar with the projects on which they are working. Whether it's through chatting or overhearing a conversation they are having with other employees, we naturally become tuned in to the general goings-on of the workplace. Although it can sometimes be considered a distraction, we actually learn a lot through these interactions.

When employees work virtually, they often miss out on the "people resources" of the on-site environment. For example, in the office, if I ask Julia a question about something and she doesn't know the answer, Ashley has the possibility to overhear what I ask and provide insight. Virtually, I can e-mail or call Julia, and she may or may not forward it on to someone else who would have a better or more complete answer.

Another example of on-site learning comes from watching others complete tasks. In an office setting, someone may see you doing a task inefficiently and contribute information on how to do it better. Virtually, there is no one there to see exactly how you are completing tasks, and you may not even realize you aren't being efficient.

A best practice to include virtual workers as people resources is to establish an online forum where employees post questions and answers. Staff members can also post tips on how they have learned to best complete various tasks. Managers can monitor posts and offer suggestions if employees' questions go unanswered.

The ability for employees to be productive while out of the office makes your business better. It extends your reach, increases the amount you can accomplish in your day, reduces your costs, and enables a healthy work/life balance. So by all means, hand your employees the right club and let them take their very best shot at success.

10. ORGANIZATIONAL CULTURE AND CORE/SHARED VALUES

This engagement driver encompasses many different elements and often plays a major role when employees consider the fit of their position. People often associate company culture with the "feel" of what it is like to be on-site at the organization. Is the atmosphere relaxed or formal? Do employees seem upbeat and enthusiastic, stressed, or as if they are walking on eggshells? There is a lot you can tell about an organization's culture by simply observing the mood of employees while they are working.

However, when all employees do not work in one location, defining culture often becomes more difficult. Employees who work from home are removed from the cultural thermometer that comes from observation. The inability to *see* culture every day in the workplace can make it more challenging for organizations to instill a sense of their culture in virtual workers. Additionally, organizations with multiple locations have the task of instilling the same cultural feel throughout the organization. For global companies where local cultures are very different, it can be challenging to uphold one company culture that is relevant to staff in all locations. How does an organization overcome such obstacles? Having a strong foundation of core/shared values is essential.

Think of values as being the compass of the working world; they lead you in the direction of where you want to go. When your employees have the same core values as your organization, they will already be headed down the path on which you are traveling. If they have different values, it will be nearly impossible to change their direction so that they follow the organization's path. This is especially relevant for virtual employees because they are generally more self-managed than employees who work in the same location as their manager. As a manager, you want to hire employees whose values have already guided them down the right path. Having shared values between employer and employees plays an essential role in establishing and upholding *the right* organizational culture.

Diversity Awareness and Inclusion

HR Solutions' Research Institute has found a strong correlation between diversity satisfaction and overall job satisfaction/engagement. It's proven that when employees feel more positively about diversity, they feel more positively about their job overall.

Global organizations have a heightened opportunity to capitalize on this engagement driver by connecting employees throughout the world. Multinational virtual teams are generally highly effective because employees bring diverse skill sets to the table and learn from one another. Employee engagement is bolstered through diverse teams, and productivity and quality often increase as well. (Chapter 6 dives into the topic of diversity in greater detail.)

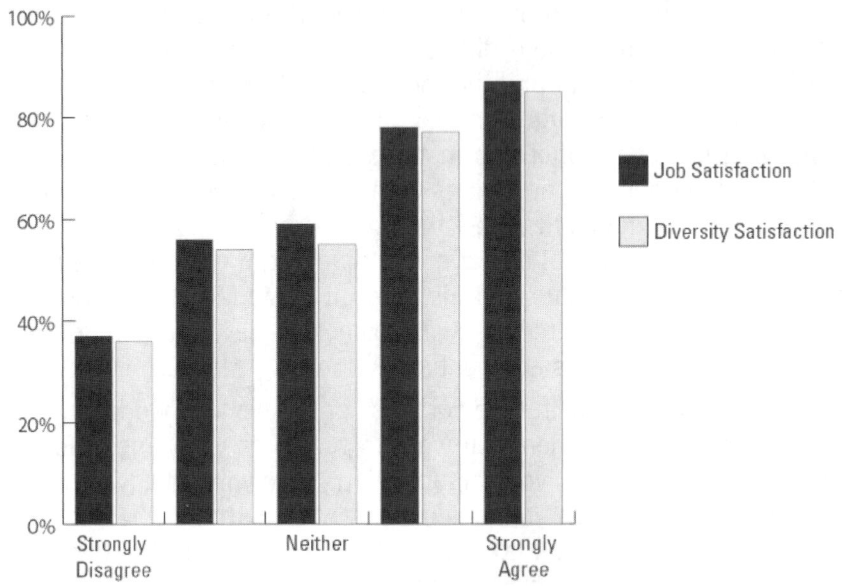

Job Satisfaction vs. Diversity Satisfaction.

Corporate Social Responsibility

Corporate social responsibility (CSR) drives engagement by showing employees their employer is making a positive impact in the world. CSR initiatives vary across companies, but the purpose is the same: to demonstrate an organization's commitment to core values through action. For virtual workers, CSR can be a powerful way to stay connected with colleagues and strengthen the employee-employer bond.

Many CSR initiatives are virtual in nature, such as fundraising for national and international nonprofits. Employees can get involved no matter where they are based, which naturally provides an even playing field for those working on-site and those working remotely. Virtual workers can spearhead CSR initiatives, allowing them to take a leadership role and collaborate with colleagues with whom they otherwise might not interact.

In addition, volunteering can be a great way for employees to see one another face to face. Companies can organize group volunteer initiatives where employees in the same area can work together and get to know one another on a more personal level. This interaction strengthens ties to the organization through supporting the strategy and mission and building coworker camaraderie.

Work/Life Balance and Workplace Flexibility

Employees' personal lives are not checked at the door when they begin the workday. Emotions and personal obligations stay with people throughout the day. A common notion is that work and personal life should be completely separated, but in reality, that is impossible; people do not transform from one person to another when they start and stop working. Trying to keep professional and personal obligations separated can actually cause added stress for employees, because personal obligations do not always fall outside the workday. When obligations overlap, it causes internal conflict for employees. Even the most engaged employees do not want to be forced to choose between doing their best at work and doing their best for their family. In this way, work/life balance includes employees' ability to have a place for their personal life *within* their work life.

The option to work virtually is an excellent way for employees to stay fully dedicated to their job without letting their personal life fall by the wayside. Do not take this to mean employees will be less productive or dedicated to their positions when their personal life isn't forced to take a hit; in fact, the aforementioned studies featured in this book have shown the opposite is true: When employees do not feel torn between their personal life and professional life, they are actually set up to succeed on the job because they have fewer distractions. Rather than worrying about juggling personal and professional responsibilities, employees can breathe easy knowing there are enough hours in the day to accomplish everything.

For many people, working from home during the hours they choose (even just a small percentage of the time) can make a resounding impact on how they view their position. This perception of increased overall value of the job opportunity certainly drives employee engagement.

As a virtual manager, it is essential to not only offer flexible work arrangements, but fully support them as well. That means when an employee requests to work remotely, as formally allowed by company policy, managers should not feel slighted by approving the arrangement. Some managers have the tendency to think employees won't work as hard when they work from home, or that employees who actively use a flex policy are less serious about their position than other employees. When managers hold these opinions, even if they keep it to themselves, employees pick up on it and feel uncomfortable using flex policies. This reaction can be damaging not only to perceptions of workplace flexibility (that is, organizational culture), but employees' relationships with direct managers as well.

In addition, when employees don't use a flex policy as much as they are permitted, another tailspin reaction is that managers erroneously assume their direct reports do not want, need, or appreciate flex options. Oftentimes, this belief leads to decreased support of flex programs until they no longer exist or add any value for employees.

In summary, there are many elements that encompass organizational culture. It can be easy for managers to presume these facets do not come into play as much in a virtual environment as for on-site employees, but that is assuredly not the case. When managers have less face-to-face contact with their direct reports, it becomes even more important to take a close look at how organizational culture is affecting engagement.

CHAPTER 6

OVERCOMING CHALLENGES: CHANGING THE LOCATION WITHOUT CHANGING ORGANIZATIONAL PRINCIPLES

Welcome to the "new normal": the distancing and separation of the virtual worker. And what a challenging new normal it is.

With virtual workforces cropping up, leadership is bound to struggle with challenges resulting from the change in organizational makeup. However, management can and will be successful in creating a flourishing virtual workforce if remote managers proactively implement appropriate strategies to keep virtual employees engaged. When managing distance teams, the trick to maintaining engagement is not solely about establishing new techniques; rather, organizational practices and policies must be altered to make them work for each unique organization and virtual workers.

The first step in implementing a successful remote team is to thoroughly consider which projects can be done virtually, as well as the estimated amount of time each task should take. Additionally, leadership must listen objectively when employees in their organization present a case for working virtually. Permitting employees to present their own individualized "virtual work plan" detailing exactly how their job is applicable to virtual work is important in creating a sense of autonomy and trust among employees, thus increasing engagement. Whereas some personalities, roles, and responsibilities truly are better suited to on-site work, management must reflect on the potential each job has to fit into the virtual world before determining suitability.

With the advent of new technology, jobs and responsibilities not originally considered suitable for the remote world are becoming more viable, so management must carefully examine each facet of a job before deciding its appropriateness for separation. For example, some people may think appointments with physicians and nurses could never be done from a distance. However, hospitals are beginning to use Webcams and other devices to reduce wait times.[1] Although there is a physical gap between physician and patient, in actuality, this method could be more personal and private: The patient would no longer be required to sit in a waiting room with 50 other people prior to being seen by the doctor. Technology creates advancements people may never have imagined, and through these developments, individuals are viewing remote work in a different way. Remote work could soon be considered suitable for almost every job.

As time goes on, virtual work will likely become less of a perk and more of an assumed aspect of many careers. As such, it is imperative that leadership fully investigates which responsibilities, employees, and positions are most suited for the virtual environment. Doing so will prepare your organization for the "new normal" of remote employment.

VIRTUAL WORK: A PRODUCT OF EXPANSION

Virtual work policies are often a product of organizational growth. Many organizations have already recognized the benefits of allowing employees to work virtually, specifically in the engagement realm. As such, these organizations currently permit some of their employees to work remotely part-time. As organizations expand, they will likely establish offices across locations, and full-time virtual work will become a necessity. Knowledge can be gleaned from allowing a small population to work remotely in order to prepare for the increasing number of virtual relationships throughout an organization.

Case Study—LinkedIn

LinkedIn operates the world's largest professional network on the Internet, with more than 120 million members in more than 200 countries and territories. Although LinkedIn does not have a formal work-from-home policy, the company allows its managers and their direct reports to establish a virtual work plan. In fact, LinkedIn provides managers with guidelines to help them assess the feasibility of working remotely when the situation arises. Although only a handful of LinkedIn's employees are currently working virtually full-time, a large majority of employees have the option to occasionally work from home.

"We are in a real growth stage as a company and have a strong bias for in-person collaboration," said Steve Cadigan, vice president of people operations at LinkedIn, who leads the organization's employee growth around the world.[2] "However, allowing our employees to work from home positively impacts engagement, gives them more freedom and flexibility to do other things, and strengthens their relationship with the company."

Building employee engagement has been top of mind for LinkedIn's senior leadership team since the company was founded in 2002. Today, the company uses its "LinkedIn Company Group" as an open forum for virtual and on-site LinkedIn employees to connect with each other as well as voice their ideas and opinions. Employees share their thoughts on what is going well in the company as well as what could work better. "The group allows us to ensure we are building a culture where our employees still feel they can raise difficult topics or subjects that may be unpopular," said Cadigan. "The open culture for us is a key to engagement and the relationship we have with our employees."

Managers at LinkedIn who oversee virtual workers understand they must go the extra mile to ensure they are providing the right amount of communication and information necessary for success. More importantly, they have a big responsibility to make sure their remote workers feel connected to the company as well as recognized. But virtual workers also have a big responsibility. "They must remember to over-communicate and make their presence known. They must also be familiar with communication technologies (i.e., Skype, instant messaging, etc.)," said Cadigan. "By using such tools regularly, employees are able to extend their ability to effectively communicate."

Open, effective communication will remain important as the company continues to experience rapid growth. In 2010, LinkedIn opened six new offices and has plans to open several more at the end of 2011. As LinkedIn expands in different cities around the world, the company is evolving to have more virtual employees outside of its corporate headquarters.

"We're building the capacity and capability of communicating with one another globally. We're in the process of building that skill set and competency," said Cadigan. "Our growth in the U.S. and globally is helping us build muscle memory with employees we do not see every day." LinkedIn's experience in allowing employees to occasionally work from home has prepared it to handle the increasing number of virtual relationships emerging throughout the world.

Challenges are guaranteed to arise as individuals switch to virtual work, but if a detailed framework, either from direct experience or through other organizations, is established, a seamless transition will be possible. Do your research. There are plenty of organizations that already have virtual work policies and can be used as an example of best practices.

COMMUNICATION: BRIDGING THE PHYSICAL GAP

As illustrated in the LinkedIn story, changing location begins, first and foremost, with recognizing the importance of communication. Communication is the *only* way to bridge the distance between remote workers, their on-site counterparts, and virtual managers. The most effective virtual teams will be built on a foundation of open and effective communication.

Constant, tailored dialogues are critical to maintaining an engaged culture, no matter where employees work. When employees are spread across various locales, communication is a necessity to maintain a connection and keep them engaged in the culture and organization. Open and effective communication will establish a link between workers in the physical office and those in the remote world.

Case Study—Brocade Communications Systems

Open, regular, and effective communication is just as important for a virtual workforce as it is for on-site managers and employees. Brocade Communications Systems, which provides reliable, high-performance network solutions to help organizations transition smoothly to a virtualized world, understands the importance such communication has for managers and their direct reports who are working virtually.

With approximately 4,700 employees worldwide, Brocade uses "Office Communicator," a live chat system, to encourage communication between managers and their virtual workers. By asking even a quick question via the online system, managers demonstrate a constant awareness of and sensitivity about keeping everyone involved.

"We remind our managers to have conversations with their virtual workers on a regular basis," said Lisa McGill, vice president of human resources at Brocade, who is responsible for leading and driving the company's strategic human resource initiatives globally.[3] "Conversation and interaction builds a strong foundation of trust. Being an inclusive manager, especially for employees who work outside the office, is essential so remote workers feel a part of the team."

To foster a virtual environment of teamwork, Brocade managers use video conferencing for their team meetings so everyone, including remote workers, can truly be there. The company also promotes the use of Webcams on its computers to enable face-to-face one-on-ones.

Brocade does not have a formal telecommuting policy, but has many employees who work remotely. Working virtually is a privilege employees can earn if they are delivering great results; the ability to work remotely can be revoked if positive results are not being delivered.

"Some people believe that if they cannot see their employees, then the work is not getting done," said McGill. "I believe that mentality needs to shift in order to remain progressive and competitive, since we have newer generations entering the workforce who absolutely have an expectation that they'll be able to telecommute as needed."

Brocade recognizes the many challenges involved in engaging a virtual workforce, such as different time zones, cultural differences, and the absence of in-person interaction. "The lack of face-to-face time is a major obstacle; however, we can still build strong relationships," said McGill. "We try to utilize video conferencing so remote workers can be seen and not just heard."

From professional development to recognition, Brocade understands the key drivers of engagement apply to a virtual workforce as well. The company created HR365, an online toolbox employees can use to create their own development plan, to help on-site staff and virtual workers figure out how they can get from their current level to a management level. Brocade also uses its "CEO Call Down" to recognize employees for a job well done. Every week, Brocade's management team is asked to provide the names of employees who do something extraordinary. Upon receiving the list, Michael Klayko, chief executive officer of Brocade, calls employees to tell them how much he appreciates them and how their actions have directly benefited the organization.

Klayko, McGill, and other Brocade employees have witnessed firsthand the benefits of a virtual workforce. Enabling employees to work remotely has helped the company use less office space, save money, increase productivity, reduce stress, and build trust. Given the fact that "Communications" is part of Brocade's name, the company has truly excelled in using the power of communication to motivate and engage *every* member of its workforce, regardless of their location.

Large, successful organizations should follow Brocade's example in realizing communication is the basis for success in the virtual world. Without effective communication methods, virtual teams will remain unconnected, and this disconnect will likely lead to the demise of the organization's virtual team. Effective virtual managers must develop a communication plan to bridge the physical gap.

In my experience, I have encountered numerous, astute best practices to help you adapt communication to create the most victorious virtual teams.

There are five types of communication around which best practices should be focused:

1. Effective communication.
2. Comprehensive communication.
3. Frequent communication.
4. Timely communication.
5. Thoughtful communication.

The following insightful tips will be extremely meaningful in bridging the gap between virtual managers and employees.

1. Effective Communication

The first step in communicating effectively is selecting the correct medium. To modify a passage from the Bible (Genesis, Chapter 1): All communication tools were not created equal. First, assess the landscape of potential tools, such as e-mail, Webinars, Webcasts, blogs, video conferences, conference calls, text, and tweets. The general rule of thumb here is to marry simple communication messages with simple communication tools. For instance, a basic notification is best served by a simple e-mail. A more complex message, which might demand interaction or the need to address concerns or answer questions, is far better suited to a video conference or Webinar.

Take the time to ask your field workers about their preferred channels of communication. For example, would they prefer e-mails, voice mail, or a live conversation? The most effective communication will be via the method on which both employees and managers agree.

Additionally, it is important to understand from whom employees would like to receive their information. As mentioned in Chapter 4, there is a disconnect between how employees receive information about their organizations and how they would *like* to receive the information. A quick win is to reduce this disconnect by creating a more open dialogue between management and virtual employees. If managers are continuously updating their team with any new developments or facts, workers will be receiving information in the way they prefer, and managers will ensure the correct information is exchanged.

At the end of virtual meetings, provide a block of time for participants to ask questions, and make it clear you are available for personal conversations pertaining to the material. Make yourself available regardless of the distance. Remote workers in various locations should know their manager will be responsive (in a timely manner) when they call to discuss anything.

Make conversation a two-way street. Virtual managers should not talk solely *at* their employees, but instead be open and active listeners as well. Encourage virtual employees to contribute thoughts, as they are likely the most aware of what is happening on their end. Persuade your remote workers to ask questions or seek clarification if need be. Make employees feel heard, and answer each and every one of their questions to the best of your ability. There is a reason employees ask questions, and it is vital managers seek answers. You may be tempted to work on other projects while on phone calls with remote employees, but keep in mind that distraction can be heard in your voice. If you can be an open listener while multitasking, that's great, but make sure employees feel they are heard. Use effective communication to vindicate virtual employees and make them feel as though you care, and they will return the feelings.

Effective communication is also clear and concise. Most of the communication between virtual managers and their employees revolves around e-mail. Writing e-mails is somewhat of an art form. As e-mails work best when they are short and to the point, one must truly consider the message he or she wants to convey. Before you hit *Send*, put yourself in the reader's shoes. Is the message long, contributing to the possibility of boredom or loss of attention? If so, shorten the e-mail as best you can. Is there a possibility the reader may misinterpret what you are trying to say? Are the spelling and grammar correct? Does the e-mail have the correct professional tone? All of these are things to be considered before circulating the message. With more than 294 billion e-mails sent on average per day,[4] a poorly written or badly proofed e-mail can bring more havoc than good.

Each person develops an e-mail "personality." By that I mean each individual has a certain *tone* in his e-mails. Virtual employees and managers must recognize that their messages convey a personality to people they may never meet face to face, and, further, the personality of each individual may be attributed to the organization as a whole: If a client is interacting with one virtual employee, and interprets this person's personality, she has a higher likelihood of thinking the entire organization is similar to this individual. Team members and managers must truly consider what personality they would like to exude. Professionalism and tone are incredibly important. It is imperative that managers understand the influence e-mails can have and encourage employees to put forth effort to convey the personality desired by management.

Example:

These two e-mails say the same thing, but consider the image in your head of the person who is writing the e-mail:

Hey there,

Wanted to say thanks for your presentation today. It was awesome. I got so much information from it, and I can't wait to use everything I learned in the future. ☺

Have a good one,

Joe

Hello Bob,

I wanted to send you a quick note to say I truly enjoyed your presentation today. It was very informative, and I left with some great knowledge I definitely plan to use in the future.

Thank you so much for taking the time to share your thoughts and research.

My best,

Joe

In my opinion, the second e-mail is much more professional. Employees will do well to act with professionalism in order to present their organization in the best way. When potential clients and customers read professionally written e-mails, they are more likely to be drawn to the organization, thinking it is on top of its game. Consider how the same thing can be said in multiple ways, and consider your audience. When in doubt, err on the side of professionalism. Managers of remote workforces should share correct techniques and tools for writing with a professional tone, so as to present their organizations in the best possible light.

Finally, managers must effectively utilize every dialogue to determine employee engagement among their virtual teams. Because virtual employees are not visible at all times, the engagement levels of virtual employees need to be discussed in depth. If you care about your remote workers' engagement levels, ask them about it. Not once a year, but on a regular basis. Astoundingly, HR Solutions' Research Institute estimates that only 5 percent of performance reviews contain a two-way dialogue about employees' engagement drivers and detractors. Why wouldn't you want to have regular check-ins with employees vis-à-vis their engagement? Not doing so is analogous to going on a diet for one day and expecting a noticeable difference when you get on the scale at the end of the month.

During these fruitful one-on-ones, simply ask the employee, "What gets you really excited and most engaged in your job? What do you find is detracting from your excitement and engagement level?"

Feed them more of the former and try to remove much of the latter. Doing so will increase engagement among employees regardless of the distance.

2. Comprehensive Communication

Think carefully about the organizational realities you know about simply because of your physical location. Whether you are in the head office or working remotely, there are aspects of your job you are aware of only through direct experience. For instance, mass e-mails may not be sent out about every minute occurrence, such as a broken printer, a sick employee, or a positive customer review. What realities might your virtual workers not know, simply because they work from home or on the road?

It is essential to establish communication methods that reach *all* members of the team, not just those on-site.

Many communication methods can be adapted to the remote environment. Take the message board in the staff room at an office, for example: It's a great method of communication among employees, but it loses its punch in the virtual world, as employees cannot see the items posted on it. However, *virtual* message boards have been created to function just like physical ones. Keeping these up-to-date and exciting will encourage members both in the physical and virtual realm to read the information.

Scheduling regular meetings and conference calls will also keep virtual workers up-to-date and involved in the organization, thereby increasing positive business outcomes. Excellent virtual managers establish and live by fairly strict protocol vis-à-vis meeting etiquette and netiquette. Ideally, agendas should be sent prior to these events. Calls, meetings, and Webinars should start on time, eliminating the commonly wasted time waiting for someone to dial in or connect. In the same vein, links and passcodes should be tested prior to the meeting. If not known in advance, take the time to introduce the participants or have them introduce themselves. For conference calls, encourage the participants to make it a habit to say their name before making a comment so that all will know from whom the comment came. Lastly, clear, professional protocol should be established with regard to who has the floor, as well as to avoid disrespectful verbal or electronic interruptions.

Great virtual managers will make a conscious attempt to include all locations, from Peoria to Peru. You might adopt a best practice of letting your locations rotate a certain responsibility, such as leading a staff meeting or sharing a success story. Rotating responsibilities will help keep each organization up-to-date on the goings-on of other locations. Such practices create a culture of inclusion as opposed to exclusion.

Effective virtual managers make a concerted effort to communicate with the team, *and* letting them communicate with one another. This is often best achieved with the use of technology; create community through the one location most everyone has in common, in spite of the separation: the Internet. Create a virtual water cooler, where employees can discuss what is happening in the office. This water cooler will encourage distance team members to remain connected with their coworkers. Schedule team lunches where food is delivered to the conference room and employees can eat together across the world via Skype or some other Webcam program. Provide places online where remote workers can go to hang out during breaks or when they want a little social exposure.

You might also consider creating a blog dedicated strictly to your remote employees. Such a blog will contribute further to creating connections and relationships among virtual employees, their coworkers, and management, leading to higher engagement among all team members.

Establishing Connections Through Internal Social Media

Many managers frown upon social media. Most discussions pertaining to Facebook, Twitter, YouTube, and MySpace focus on what should and should not be blocked within the office environment. These discussions result from the rise in popularity of these sites. As younger generations enter the workplace in large numbers, the cohort of employees who are Internet- and technology-savvy continues to grow. As such, social media platforms are especially impactful among this population. Management should stop fighting social media; rather, embrace it and adapt it to fit the needs of a virtual workforce.

Large, global organizations have begun to use social media to their advantage, providing a link between various locations across the world. Here are a few examples:

- To establish a community despite the distance between its members, leadership at Sabre Holdings, a global travel and tourism organization, created Sabre Town. With employees spread across 59 countries worldwide, the social media platform allows employees to feel connected regardless of their location. Users are encouraged to create a profile containing their picture, title, location, contact information, and personal data such as hometown and where they like to travel. More than 90 percent of Sabre Holdings's 10,000 employees are connected through Sabre Town.[5]
- McDonalds launched StationM, an internal social media platform aimed at connecting crews, managers, and executives throughout

the 119 countries where McDonalds is located. Employees can post content and comment on a variety of topics, including products, promotions, and operations. Team members with different backgrounds can connect with each other, and everyone's voices can be heard. Since its inception, StationM has continued to grow, with 3,000 to 4,000 unique users per month.[6]

Platforms such as Sabre Town and StationM are available to employees working in the field who can glean information about the organization from these sites regardless of their locations. Additionally, any other employees who do not necessarily have access to computers all day can utilize these platforms to stay connected. Best practices and success stories can be shared across locations, contributing to a culture of recognition and success. Employees can use the system to join groups and establish bonds with like-minded individuals. In this way, they can establish True North Groups, a term coined by Bill George, co-author of *True North*. True North Groups are groups of individuals who have similar perspectives and talk openly with each other about opportunities and concerns in a confidential environment. Remote employees can utilize social media platforms to connect and discuss their personal strengths and weaknesses, as well as any issues they are facing in the virtual environment, by creating True North Groups. Workers can pose questions and get answers from a variety of different people, thus ensuring more well-rounded information. Although they may never meet the coworkers with whom they interact, virtual communities help the organization to feel smaller despite the large distance between locations.

Organizations should utilize the tools they have available to establish and maintain strong connections. Every communication method should be inclusive, so as to nurture dialogues and channels of information that reach every member of the team. In this way, virtual employees will not miss out on information simply because they are not present in the on-site office. Comprehensive communication is critical to inclusion.

3. Frequent Communication

Here's another best practice: frequency, frequency, frequency. Remote workforces require an even greater amount of communication than their cohorts in the home office. Employees may begin to feel lost if not kept up-to-date on the status of an organization. They also lose a sense of culture, because they are not necessarily part of organizational conversations. It is essential to communicate with remote workers frequently to keep them involved and engaged. Essentially, keep communicating until they ask you to stop.

Coinciding with the need for more communication, virtual managers need to check in more often with employees. In an office setting, management can observe the physical cues of their employees. If someone is sulking around the office, a manager has the opportunity to view this and (being the good leader he is) ask the employee why she looks so upset or stressed. However, when team members are working virtually, this is unfortunately not the case. If an employee is struggling, managers are less likely to see this and realize the necessity of working to correct the problem. In order to manage this imbalance, conversations should focus on more than simply the progress an employee has made. Managers should ask questions that relate to how the employee is feeling, really digging deep into each team member's status. Further, virtual employees need to be forthright and willing to share their feelings, not relying solely on management to see that something is amiss.

Supervisors should also establish communication around workloads. Often, when a new responsibilities arise, it is easy to assign it to the first person the manager encounters. To tailor this challenge to the virtual workforce, employers need to be extra aware of employees' given tasks, and continue to monitor employees' progress on projects. Additionally, employees working virtually need to take the initiative to tell managers when they desire additional projects. Then, when new projects arise, leaders will have a better idea of the workloads of each employee, and they will be more likely to assign a new project to someone with a lighter workload. Communication such as this will also increase the chance that managers will become aware of what each particular employee enjoys doing, and will therefore be more likely to assign tasks employees find enjoyable. This way, team members will be more engaged in their projects, thereby contributing to greater business success.

4. Timely Communication

Another great communication tenet for the virtual manager is this: "Make sure you always respond to your virtual employee.

If you simply read or hear his message and hit *Delete*, you will be unknowingly fueling the flames of his personal state of separation. A manager's non-responsiveness creates blanks or virtual black holes in communication, which many remote workers will interpret as negative, due to assumptions, confusion, or just simple insecurity. Virtual employees want to know what's going on, and ignoring their messages will make them feel lost.

Conversely, by responding to every e-mail, text, tweet, and voice mail, and doing so in a timely manner, you are consistently reminding virtual employees of how connected they are, and also of how much you care about them. To use a baseball analogy, these consistent singles lead to regular game wins and, ultimately, a winning season.

Webcams can bring great effectiveness to the virtual manager. Use of video conferencing and cameras in the business world is expected to increase by 13 to 15 percent in coming years,[7] becoming more common than other communication tools such as text messaging, social media, and mobile phones. Not only do Webcams require timely responses and more natural communication patterns, you can actually *see* the people you are managing, thereby eradicating the challenges of the "now you see me, now you don't" virtual environment. The camera should in no way be powered on at all times; doing so reduces the feelings of trust and autonomy advanced through virtual work. However, Webcams are ideal for meetings and video conferencing, or one-on-one communications with virtual employees. The very fact there is a face in the picture brings a much more emotional and caring feel to the communication. Note to the virtual worker: Don't forget to change out of your pajamas.

Timely communication between coworkers is equally as important. Managers need to ensure all of their employees are responding to internal messages in an appropriate amount of time. Imagine you are working on a project, and you need information from another team member in order to complete it. You e-mail the individual, but he does not respond. You try calling, but there is no answer and he does not call you back. When you work in the same office, it is easy to stop by and see a coworker in person, but physical communication is often not an option among virtual employees, and unresponsiveness may thus be a more common occurrence. When coworkers do not respond in a timely manner to requests, their virtual counterparts will likely become frustrated and feel a loss of control, leading to higher rates of disengagement. Management should resolve this issue up-front by establishing correct protocols for communication across the board.

5. Thoughtful Communication

Effective virtual managers must always be genuine and thoughtful in what they say. Employees value specific traits and characteristics in communication, and recognizing these attributes will contribute to the best communication practices. HR Solutions' Research Institute has conducted thousands of surveys and focus groups on communication-related topics. Some of the most insightful themes that emerged from this research are as follows:

Communication Traits Most Appreciated in the Workplace

- Honesty.
- Respect.
- Politeness.
- Thoughtfulness.
- Professionalism.
- An engaging topic.
- Clear, concise, and factual communication.
- Patience.
- Objectivity.
- Tolerance of different points of view.
- Fairness.

Equally as important, and perceptive, is the flip side:

Detrimental Communication Traits in the Workplace

- Dishonesty.
- Disrespect.
- Rudeness.
- Too much or too little detail.
- Long-winded explanations.
- Lack of focus and direction.
- Lack of clarity.

- Interruptions.
- Condescension.
- Rushed communication.
- Lack of openness to other ideas.
- One-sided communication.
- Yelling and other aggressive behavior.

Virtual managers should consider these traits—both good and bad—and incorporate this knowledge into their communication techniques. Each trait can and will be apparent in *any* form of communication, be it written, vocal, or through physical cues. Before sending e-mails or communicating with virtual employees, ensure the dialogue includes more of the first list and less of the second.

In addition, *make it personal*. Remember: Your virtual employees are longing to feel *connected*. Remote workers badly want to know that their manager truly cares about them. They are yearning for this type of attention and interaction. Thus, the most effective virtual managers will take the time to ask employees what is going on in their personal lives and/or their local communities or states. Some of this type of interaction is even more effective if used during group conference calls, video conferences, or Webinars.

Have individual conversations with each team member. Encourage them to come to you if they have concerns, problems, or some issue that is creating a degree of disengagement. Let them know that you are always there to listen and that you value and welcome any ideas or suggestions they may have. Sending this positive message is one more way of widening the two-way street and enhancing relationship connectivity.

Finally, one of the greatest, most meaningful defining moments of communication between the virtual manager and employee is when the employee is faced with a family or personal crisis. It is at exactly this moment that great virtual managers shine, and shine brightly. During conversations surrounding these occurrences, remote leaders show kindness, understanding, and connectivity to the person's dilemma. Maybe these opportunities are missed by managers because of a lesser physical and emotional connection. As such, managers may not be as in tune to the everyday occurrences of their individual workers. However, if virtual managers make it a point to encourage conversations to be more personal, as well as continually read outside the lines, they are more likely to realize when something is wrong with an employee. Provide support if the worker is experiencing a troubled marriage, major job stress, an imbalance of work/family life, or all of the above. The bottom line best practice compass for awesome virtual managers is: Do the right thing. You would be surprised how many miss the opportunity and don't seize the moment by doing what is right.

All of the great advice in the previous paragraphs can be thrown out the window if your communication and concern is not *Genuine* with a capital G. Your messaging must be both honest and sincere, and any attempt to fake it will be clearly transparent to your employees; they are simply too smart not to see the phoniness.

Effective, comprehensive, timely, and most importantly, Genuine conversation is *the* most important way to bridge the gap between the main office and virtual employees. It is the basis for success, no matter how you look at it.

Without communication, it is impossible to create a connection between remote workers and management. This missing connection will contribute to disengaged virtual workers who will ultimately fail.

WHEN WORKING VIRTUALLY IS AN OPTION FOR ONLY SOME

"But it's not fair!"

As a father, I hear these words quite often. One daughter receives a privilege the other desires, and chaos ensues.

Although you probably will not hear this exact phrase as a virtual manager, I can assure you that you will encounter employees who feel a sense of unfairness at being "stuck" in the office. Different roles and personalities require different settings, so every employee will not have the ability to work at a distance. Some employees, however, may not recognize why they must remain on-site, and a negative mindset will result. This mentality contributes to disengagement through:

- Micromanagement.
- Jealousy.
- Unresponsiveness.
- Perceived workload.

Micromanagement

Employees who remain in the physical office might believe they are not as trusted and do not have as much autonomy as their virtual peers.

Think back to when you were a child: Remember when your parents or guardians finally allowed you to stay at home without a babysitter while they went out for the night? This responsibility is often a part of growing up, and the feelings of freedom and trust that result are similar to what an employee experiences when permitted to work virtually. Employees who do not receive this privilege will likely think management wants to watch their every move, not trusting them to do their work without supervision. As a result, workers will develop a "Big Brother is watching you" mentality, causing heightened stress from the constant observation or scrutiny of their work.

When employees are always being observed, they may think they are being micromanaged. They are less apt to contribute ideas or take chances that might result in better business outcomes.[8] The fact that they are in the office with somewhat-constant supervision will contribute to the belief that they must do projects and assignments a certain way. They may become lost in the bureaucracy of the organization, and, rather than exerting extra effort, do just enough to get by. Creativity and innovation are thus greatly limited.

Additionally, micromanagement contributes to a follower mentality. Employees are encouraged to ask for help and be passive rather than make their own decisions and have confidence in these decisions. These learned behaviors of constantly reporting to someone further limit creativity and "out of the box" ideas. When you are consistently guided and told to do projects a certain way, you will be less likely to come up with new, and possibly better methods to complete the project.

Jealousy

Being required to work on-site may create jealousy stemming from the perceived privileges virtual employees receive. These jealous feelings may in turn foster resentment. Once resentment is rooted, employees will likely be hard-pressed to go above and beyond on the job, falling victim to their internal beliefs. Resentment may cause employees to treat virtual coworkers with less respect, and coworker satisfaction may suffer. As coworker satisfaction is critical in retention, virtual managers must stop the green-eyed monster in order to keep employees engaged and retain them despite their location.

Unresponsiveness

People are forgetful by nature. That is part of the reason photographic memories and individuals with exceptional recall skills are looked upon with such amazement. In the office, employees are often working on multiple projects at once while trying to keep up to date on their e-mails, phone calls, and other priorities. Sometimes, responsibilities simply slip our minds.

For example, you get a request from a coworker to review a document. However, as the day becomes busy, you are stretched thin, and the coworker's document is pushed from your mind. The team member then walks by your office, and you are visually reminded about your promise. You promptly review the document and return it to your friend.

When working virtually, these visual reminders are not present. On-site team members may simply forget about requests made by virtual counterparts—not intentionally, but due to the nature of humans and the office setting. Virtual workers may view this forgetfulness as an affront when, in actuality, it is merely an accident.

Unresponsiveness, even by accident, leads to frustration among remote workers and in-office counterparts alike, as distance communication is virtually the only way team members in all locations can connect. Negative standpoints on both ends of the equation will create a decrease in morale, leading to a cycle of disengagement. Virtual workers must be proactive, explicitly reminding the on-site employee about their request, as they cannot simply wait for the employee to remember.

Perceived Workload

Employees in the office may also become preoccupied with an idea of workload fairness. When working on-site, employees tend to adopt the mindset many managers use: If a coworker is present, she is likely working. However, as mentioned previously, this "visual check" is not applicable to remote workers, and employees in the office may think they are doing more than others because they cannot *see* virtual team members physically working. As such, on-site employees may think they are contributing a greater amount to the organization, but not receiving the same privileges as those employees who are working at a distance. They also might view remote workers as slacking off, leaving more responsibility to workers in the office.

THE BENEFITS OF REMAINING ON-SITE

Throughout this book, I have outlined, in depth, the benefits of working virtually, but in establishing engagement among all employees, it is equally as essential to highlight the benefits of remaining on-site. To reduce perceptions of unfairness and disengagement, effective remote employers should:

- Communicate, communicate, communicate.
- Create a detailed virtual work plan.
- Maintain workload fairness.
- Offer parallel benefits to employees remaining on site.
- Provide creative time.

Communication

Employees will ask questions such as "What is it about Bob that makes him suitable to work from home?" or "I have plenty of responsibilities I can easily do remotely. Why can't I work outside the office?" Each of these questions is a legitimate inquiry, and each should be addressed appropriately.

Begin with communication. Create a two-way dialogue detailing exactly why you believe employees should remain in the office, and work to understand their reasoning for wanting to work remotely. Emphasize the critical importance of working on-site to fulfill the employee's particular job duties or fit the employee's personality. It is important to make the employee understand that his ability to contribute to the organization's success will be better aligned with an in-office job. When explaining why an employee should work on-site, think positively. Do *not* say, "You can't work virtually because you are not self-motivated"; rather, "You work better in a group, so the physical office setting is more suited for you."

Highlight the numerous benefits provided by remaining on-site. One such benefit is the separation of work and home life that a physical office creates: On-site employees may have more of an opportunity to leave work at work, because they are physically leaving an office at a set time. Virtual workers, on the other hand, may always be connected, because they do not necessarily have a physical indicator for when they are not at work.

An additional benefit to the on-site office is the ability to brainstorm live with coworkers. When stuck on a problem or confused about a project, on-site employees can simply stop by a team member's office and ask a question or talk face-to-face about a problem, and a better solution will likely result. Virtual employees, on the other hand, will likely perform this process via e-mail or over the phone, which may not be as conducive to brainstorming.

Most importantly, relationship development may be easier on-site. Face-to-face interactions are more prevalent, contributing to quicker relationship formation. You can simply stop by a coworker's office and invite her to lunch, or just pop in to chat. Conversations are less work-focused when interacting face-to-face, and friendships can more easily develop. On-site employees might be more satisfied with their coworkers, and therefore, as coworker satisfaction is the unsung hero of retention, be more likely to remain with the organization.

A Virtual Work Plan

Developing and communicating a comprehensive action plan for virtual work is the foundation for establishing fairness despite the distance. If guidelines are presented clarifying exactly when and how an employee can work virtually, and these guidelines are shared with the team, employees who remain in the office will be more likely to understand why they cannot work remotely. The more if/then statements you provide to employees through this action plan, the less ambiguity will be present, and employees will be more likely to see the rationale behind keeping them on-site. Team members can also use these guidelines as personal goals—if their jobs are suitable for virtual work, but they are not permitted to work remotely, they can adapt their work habits accordingly.

Workload Fairness

Consistently balance workloads between employees working remotely and those in the physical office. You may benefit from establishing a shared database outlining the amount of work each individual is doing so misperceptions do not arise. Employees can consult this database whenever they please, so as to better understand everyone's exact workload. Continue to assign projects based on employees' likes and dislikes, in order to encourage engagement despite one's physical location. Assigning projects employees enjoy will make it less likely for them to feel they are receiving greater amounts of work. Doesn't it seem easier to accomplish something you enjoy rather than something you do not?

Parallel Benefits

Employees working in the physical office location may not have as much time as virtual workers to handle daily, personal tasks, such as washing clothes or making lunches. Effective virtual managers should offer concierge services that allow on-site employees to manage their personal tasks. Dry cleaning services, personal grocery shopping, and on-site daycare are examples of benefits on-site employees will appreciate.

Implementing a casual dress code in the office will often be an easy win for virtual managers as well. Doing so will reduce a small but important discrepancy between virtual employees and their on-site counterparts. Additionally, flex hours can be instituted if employees' jobs do not lend themselves to working remotely. Commuting costs should be covered so as to reduce any financial strain resulting from working in the office. Each of these practices seems simple, but providing employees with these benefits will negate the idea that virtual employees receive more privileges.

Creative Time

Effective virtual managers can decrease any perception of micromanagement and lost freedom by providing set "creative time" for employees. At Google, for example, leadership encourages employees to spend 20 percent of their time devoted to problems of their own choosing. In providing this opportunity, employees contribute ideas and innovation to Google. With creative time, team members will be aware of the freedom and autonomy they have to provide outcomes for the organization. As such, they are likely to remain engaged. Effective virtual managers could follow Google's example to increase feelings of autonomy for on-site employees.

There is no "i" in "team," and in keeping with this message, virtual managers need to recognize the importance of *all* of their employees, both on site and at a distance. Engaging each and every one of them will contribute to the strongest and most beneficial foundation for success. Providing privileges and establishing rules will help reduce any internal petulant child murmurings of "it's not fair" among on-site and virtual workers alike, and keep employees across locations truly dedicated, invested, and engaged.

DIVERSITY IN THE VIRTUAL ENVIRONMENT

As part of their very nature, virtual teams span locations, and thus, they innately include individuals from different cultures, societies, and backgrounds. A great amount of diversity is an unavoidable outcome of virtual teams. Research has found a strong correlation between diversity

satisfaction and engagement. The most successful virtual managers will recognize this link and will put forth effort to effectively create a culture of not just acceptance, but *inclusion* across all backgrounds.

Diversity is the big elephant in the virtual room. Although remote employees frequently interact with coworkers of different backgrounds, they shy away from every mention of diversity or difference, because individuals are often raised to avoid these discussions.

However, the distanced nature of virtual work *requires* diversity to be a conversation piece. Actively recognizing the various generations and cultural groups within the virtual workforce, along with the benefits and challenges each group brings, will help create a thriving and engaged remote team.

Generational Differences

Bob Dylan was correct when he sang, "The times they are a-changing." With the advancements technology and innovation bring, interactions among members of the workforce change. Currently, four generations are working side by side in the workplace: Traditionalists, Baby Boomers, Generation X, and Millennials. Each generation presents unique and varied views of working virtually. A one-size-fits-all approach will not create an effective virtual team.

Traditionalists

Traditionalists are those employees born between 1929 and 1946. Their childhoods were colored by economic uncertainty, resulting from events such as the Great Depression and World War II. Although more prosperous times came later in life, their backgrounds contributed to their strong work ethic and financial conservatism.

Employees in the Traditionalist cohort value hard work, accountability, duty, and sacrifice. They have a strong sense of respect for authority and the government. They believe recognition and promotions come with job tenure. To Traditionalists, a job is "work," not intended to be enjoyable; rather, they seek personal fulfillment through other channels. They are incredibly loyal to their organization, and this loyalty keeps them devoted regardless of where they are working.

Engagement Drivers:

- Senior management's relationship with employees.
- Strategy and mission—especially the freedom and autonomy to succeed and contribute to the organization's success.

Traditionalists are attracted to the possibility of retiring gradually through virtual work. With their work ethic and devotion to their employer, most Traditionalists do not want to simply stop working when they retire. Rather, many would prefer to work part-time, still contributing to the organization. Through virtual work, these employees can maintain ties with their employer while transitioning.

Traditionalists may have difficulty in switching from a more conventional work environment to the flexibility in location and hours offered in the remote world. Many Traditionalists have been working for more than 50 years in an office with set hours and a chain of command. They are likely most comfortable with face-to-face meetings and conversations, and may have a hard time adapting to working with individuals they cannot see. Effective virtual managers will outline policies to help Traditionalists recognize the structure of the organization despite being removed from the on-site office.

Baby Boomers

Baby Boomers are those employees born between 1947 and 1965. They are the generation of music, opportunities, and innovation. They were captivated as man took his first step on the moon, experienced Woodstock firsthand, and watched people of all backgrounds fight for equal rights.

These employees are strong believers in teamwork and building relationships with others. They value equal opportunity. They are encouraged by financial success, and hold the mentality of "spend now, worry later." These team members "live to work," revolving their lives around their careers. Their occupations are part of their identity. Boomers are not job-hoppers; they often devote their entire lives to a certain organizations. Many believe Boomers were the original "workaholics": they enjoy working to achieve their dreams, and are willing to put forth extra effort to get there, even if it means working more hours.

Engagement Drivers:

- Career development.
- Job content—the ability to do what I do best.

Similar to Traditionalists, Boomers will value the opportunity to retire gradually. Because they often "live to work," employees in this group will cherish being able to continue working despite growing older. Additionally, Boomers appreciate virtual work because it allows them to reduce burnout. Their focus on their careers often contributes to high levels of stress and constant action, thus creating a higher chance of becoming overwhelmed and overburdened. When permitted to work virtually, Boomers may be able to create a better balance between working hard and working too much.

As remote workers, late Boomers might be largely concerned with how to advance in their careers when working from a distance. They may see career growth as stagnant, as they are not visible to management and thus can only be judged based on their output and not their personality. Management may not be aware of these employees' leadership qualities, as their interactions with coworkers are never observed. Boomers may also not have the opportunity to observe other roles that may be of interest to them when they are isolated in their own office or across the world. Effective virtual managers must ensure Boomers know they will have the opportunity to advance despite the distance. Provide career courses and personal development so Boomers feel they are advancing. Create protocols for advancement that clearly outline how to move around in the organization, so Boomers are aware of what they need to do.

Generation Xers

Generation Xers were born between 1966 and 1972. They experienced the *Challenger* shuttle explosion, the fall of the Berlin Wall, and the Feminist Movement. They are individuals who grew up in a time of high divorce rates and the decrease of the nuclear family, which contributed to their adaptable and flexible natures.

These individuals are the "latchkey" generation—children returning home from school to empty houses while their parents finished work for the day. They are self-reliant, independent, and resourceful. In the work environment, they often want to be left alone to do their work. Xers are a group that values a focus on results—ideal for the virtual world, where results are the main performance indicator.

Engagement Drivers:

- Strategy and mission—especially the freedom and autonomy to succeed and contribute to the organization's success.
- Open and effective communication.

Because Xers are independent and often want to be left to their own devices, they are drawn to the virtual world; it gives them their desired freedom and self-sufficiency. They do not need a lot of direction from management, and thus are ideal for the remote realm, where direct supervision may be minimal. Generation X will thrive with a lack of direct and constant supervision.

Generation Xers are also drawn to the work/life balance offered through virtual work. In contrast to past generations, Xers do not view their work as indicative of their worth. Careers do not define who they are; they see work as *one part* of their lives, rather than the single most important aspect. Virtual work provides Xers with more opportunity to establish lives outside of their jobs.

When working virtually, Xers may not be as cognizant of their contribution to the "big picture" and the overall outcome within the organization. As such, they may fee undervalued. When you are in an on-site office, you are more likely to see how your work plays into the work of others and the organization; however, working virtually limits access to visually observing the difference each of your actions can have. The isolation one feels while working in a separated location may further contribute to not feeling like part of the overall outcome of the organization. As a result, Generation Xers may be less drawn to virtual work because their contribution and value are not as overt. Management must do everything in its power to stress the role the employee plays in the organization, despite the distance.

Millennials

Millennials are employees born between 1980 and 1992. They grew up in the age of the Internet, technology, and the War on Terror. They are the generation of helicopter parents—those who seem to constantly "hover" over their children—and constant guidance. Instant gratification and recognition are standard for these individuals. Thus, Millennials value constant communication and direction. Having been involved in countless activities in their youth, they thrive when regularly switching from one activity to another. In essence, they are professional multitaskers. In a reversal from earlier generations, trust and loyalty to an organization must be *earned* rather than simply assumed.

Engagement Drivers:

- Recognition.
- Organizational culture and core/shared values.
- Coworker satisfaction—the unsung hero of retention.

Similar to Boomers, Millennials are attracted to virtual work for the work/life balance it offers. Millennials have a "work to live" mentality, more so than past generations. They largely work so they can enjoy other aspects of their lives. Their tendency to multitask spreads beyond childhood, and often as adults they are involved in a large number of personal and professional activities. Virtual work provides more discretionary time for each of their various affairs.

Millennials also appreciate the effect virtual work has on organizational culture. Employees in this cohort are incredibly dedicated to corporate social responsibility, resulting from volunteering through school and extracurricular activities their entire lives. Not only does virtual work provide them with more personal time to volunteer, but the positive environmental benefits it provides are also strong attractors for this group.

Because they desire step-by-step processes and protocols, working virtually may be a challenge for Millennials. They are a generation that has been guided every step of the way, and they are most comfortable when they know exactly what needs to be done and how to do it. In communication via e-mail, instructions may not be as explicit, and Millennials may struggle with less comprehensive guidelines. Effective virtual managers must make clear exactly what they are expecting when allowing employees to work remotely. Additionally, virtual employees in the Millennial group must make a concerted effort to ask all the questions they need to know, both prior to beginning a project and along the way.

Virtual managers *will* encounter resistance and questions when permitting employees of different generations to work virtually. Leverage each generation's particular engagement driver in order to successfully keep engagement alive across the different cohorts and locations.

Let's Talk About Tech

"You can't teach an old dog new tricks."

This saying doesn't hold nearly as much truth as people tout, but it does contain a warning—one that virtual managers should abide by:

Generations approach technology in different ways. For instance, many Millennials often have never known a world without technology. They grew up using phones with caller ID, are more familiar with Wikipedia than encyclopedias, and may not know the origin of the phrase "like a broken record." Traditionalists, on the other hand, often had to hand-write memos and re-type documents to fix one minor mistake. Gone are the days when you had to arrange a meeting place in advance and commute to that location; now you can simply call someone from home, the office, or the park, and video chat on your iPhone. Each generation must approach technology as a learning experience in the workforce, and adapt in various ways.

It is a commonly held stereotype that Traditionalists are less adept with technology, because they did, at one point, live in a time when computers and the World Wide Web did not exist. This stereotype, like most, does not tell the full story, as Traditionalists are often more proficient with technology than many people realize. Some individuals in the Traditionalist generation may indeed not understand how to use various devices, but others may know even more than the IT department. Thus, virtual managers must work closely with individuals from all generations to understand exactly what they know and what they can stand to gain.

Additionally, use of technology is not simply understanding the basics, but understanding *appropriateness*. With the role technology plays in their personal lives, Millennials may not comprehend the different approaches to technology they must employ in the work environment. The short and constant status updates on Facebook and Twitter, the use of "ur" for "you are," and inserting smiley faces or other "emoticons" into correspondence are not conducive to the professionalism required within the workforce. Successful virtual managers should offer guidance, classes, and training for effective technology use. Every generation can benefit from continued learning, especially as it relates to the ever-changing virtual work environment.

Cultural Differences

An organization with virtual employees is bound to skirt geographical boundaries in some way. The social norms of different cultures are likely to collide; the question is whether an explosion or a magnificent combination will result.

Language Barriers

One recent survey found that language presented one of the greatest general hurdles to virtual teams, with 64 percent of respondents highlighting this challenge.[9] Virtual communication is already more challenging than face-to-face communication; add in language differences, and you may have a whole other ball game.

There are many reasons language barriers present a challenge: Phrases do not necessarily translate directly, accents often affect pronunciation or make it more difficult to understand what is being said, and slang, clichés, and dialects change messages. Even within the same country, words vary based on the area. Do you call it pop, soda, or Coke? Bubbler or water fountain? Encourage virtual workers to be clear and concise, and discourage the use of slang or clichés, which may be misinterpreted. Virtual employees must recognize how complicated language is, and how seemingly "basic" messages may be confusing to the recipient.

Effective virtual managers will proactively identify the impact language barriers could make, and mentor their employees on how to handle any challenges. Offer training courses for employees to learn new languages if they so desire. Becoming proficient in various conversational languages can have a large influence on communication and teamwork. Providing workers with the knowledge of how exactly language may affect their interactions will allow them to be more prepared and become better communicators.

Collectivist vs. Individualist Cultures

Every person is a product of the societal norms of his background. Different cultures have different norms for interactions and work ethic. Countries such as the United States and Canada are individualist cultures; rather than group efforts and teamwork, individual success is valued. Collectivist cultures, on the other hand, are focused more on the group; what is good for the team is good for each individual. Individualism is about getting ahead on your own and working your way to the top; collectivism is about doing what's best for everyone involved, even if it means making personal sacrifices.

Employees often make decisions based on their personal schema. For example, employees who were raised in a collectivist culture, learning the phrase "the nail that sticks out gets hammered down," will likely have less inclination to make decisions that will distinguish them from the group. Employees raised from an individualist background, where "you shouldn't allow anything to stand in your way," will make choices based on what helps them personally advance. Explaining how decisions were made will thus be more difficult when communicating across cultures, as factors in the decision will be weighed differently, leading to disagreement. Collectivist cultures also may struggle with virtual work, especially working remotely and in isolation, as they are more comfortable with group efforts.

Virtual managers must create a culture within their organization that marries individualist and collectivist cultures. Combine beliefs held by both types of employees, and create a middle ground so both are content. Additionally, virtual managers must recognize the foundation from which *they* were raised, and keep this in mind when interacting with individuals across cultures. Awareness will lead to fairness.

Further contributing to cultural differences, holidays, vacations, religions, and societal norms all factor in to interactions across locations. When entire offices in one country are closed due to a national holiday, another location within the organization may continue to be working away at the daily grind. Productivity could be limited as a result, especially if an employee in the open office needs something from a coworker in the closed office. Virtual managers can mitigate this issue by preparing in advance for any closures. Virtual employees themselves must also be proactive when closures are approaching, and ask for the information they think they will need ahead of time. Further, every holiday and observance must be recognized as legitimate and important, regardless of the virtual manager's own beliefs. Many offices are closed on Christmas, but employees observing Ramadan, Hanukah, or another religious holiday will likely value additional time off, as these holidays do not necessarily fall on December 25th. Virtual managers should offer floating holidays so multinational teams can have the same paid-time-off benefits. Fostering a culture where everyone is permitted to observe their beliefs will keep employees engaged and committed to their organization.

Effective virtual managers can reconcile generational and cultural differences by clearly understanding employees' backgrounds. Implement classes and activities aimed at encouraging employees across locations and generations to understand each other. When management works to create a culture of inclusion by encouraging employees across generations to be open-minded and willing to learn, and incorporating policies to aid in diversity satisfaction, engagement will result.

Virtual managers will face challenges in transitioning to a virtual workforce, but approaching them armed with the knowledge and techniques presented by this book will allow you to overcome any roadblocks. You *can* change the location without changing organizational principles. Being an effective virtual manager requires proactive knowledge. You're already heading in the right direction. After all, you *are* reading this book.

CHAPTER 7

MANAGING PEOPLE YOU CAN'T SEE

There are countless situations in which employees work virtually, so of course there are differing perspectives on the experience. As with most things in life, there are aspects of working remotely that are perceived as being more positive, and others that could be considered more challenging. As a virtual manager, is it important for you to understand how these elements affect your employees' experience on a day-to-day basis, as well as through time.

Because you are generally physically separated from these workers, you will need to work harder to fully understand what it is like to be in their shoes. I assure you, it is worth the time and effort to build this understanding. Without ascertaining what working virtually is like at *your* organization, you will not be able to effectively motivate, engage, and retain your employees.

TRAINING, LEARNING, DEVELOPMENT

The transition from working in the office every day to having a remote role can be tricky for employees and their managers. Unfortunately, training for both remote managers and employees on how to work and manage virtually is often overlooked. According to a study from World at Work, only 21 percent of employers provide training to managers on how to implement and support virtual work programs, and just 17 percent offer training to employees on how to be successful virtual employees.[1] Proper training is essential to building a strong virtual team.

Case Study: Teach for America

One organization that does a great job training its virtual workforce is Teach for America. Teach for America (TFA) has gained popularity and notoriety since it was founded in 1990 thanks to its mission to bring excellent education to every child in America. However, what most people don't realize about TFA is that it relies heavily on a virtual workforce to organize and manage its program participants (known as corps members), who are located across the country.

TFA has seen exponential growth in the past decade. When Aimée Eubanks Davis became the chief people officer in 2005, she oversaw the organization's staff grow from 200 to more than 1,500 staff members. Eubanks Davis credits much of their success to the staff's ability to work virtually. "We simply would not be able to attract the caliber of talent that we do if we were not flexible on location," she said.[2] Staff members not only work from more than 40 in-region offices, but also from home in cities across the country. In fact, 10 of their 12 leadership team members live in different cities. Some staff members started off as virtual employees, and others were able to begin working remotely after relocating, allowing them to stay on staff. "The biggest benefit [of employing virtual workers] is that we are able to attract and retain folks who we simply otherwise could not if we imposed geographic limitations," said Eubanks Davis.

In order to ensure their virtual team is working as efficiently as possible, Eubanks Davis includes remote managing into their new hire training. Managers learn the best ways to communicate with employees (e-mail isn't always the best option), as well as complete self-paced trainings to learn about virtual management, building and sustaining trust, clarifying team roles and connecting responsibilities to the organization's strategy and mission, identifying and responding to employee motivators, giving feedback to remote employees, and developing personal operating systems. TFA's e-library also includes a number of resources about managing in a virtual environment.

TFA utilizes a number of techniques to reach its virtual workforce. Much of their work is done virtually through conference calls, online meetings, and Webinars. To communicate with the employee base as a whole, the leadership team hosts a virtual event called "The Blank Show," which works as a virtual town meeting. During the show, senior leaders discuss company news and new initiatives, and highlight inspirational stories from corps members. In addition, TFA uses Yammer, an internal social media application that allows staff members to interact virtually. Employees are encouraged to share quick wins and best practices, recognize each other's work, share news, and interact in smaller groups based on employee roles, interests, and backgrounds.

TFA's virtual workforce has allowed it to accomplish some amazing things in just 20 years, including being included on the Fortune 100 Best Places to work list. With TFA's growing alumni base of more than 33,000 former corps members who are actively advocating for the program and joining their staff, Teach for America—as well as the United States's education system—is in for a bright future.

Manager Training

Training for first-time remote managers is extremely important, because virtual employees cannot succeed if their managers aren't leading successfully. Management training should focus on several areas:

- Project management and management processes: Can include information on making sure that work is completed, tracking systems, and effective use of technology.

- Communication techniques: connecting with employees; the best scenarios for using different types of technology; communicating across time zones, languages, and other barriers; and proper tone and other nonverbal cues.
- Team coordination and management: building trust among team members as well as clearly identifying and assigning employee roles and responsibilities.
- Employee motivation: Should include information about identifying and amplifying individual employee motivators.
- Strategy and mission: managers should learn to connect employee performance and outcomes to the organization's strategy and mission.
- Performance management: recognizing employees, making sure employees know what they are doing well and areas for improvement, and delivery of employee feedback.

For remote managers, a best practice is to conduct training virtually, either internally or using an external vendor. Not only does this allow managers to focus on areas that are most useful to them and train at their own pace, but it also gives them some insight into what it is like to work virtually. This insight will help managers better understand any challenges employees may face when working remotely.

Employee Training

Transitioning Employees to the Virtual Workplace

Many employees who have worked successfully for years in traditional workplaces have a hard time adapting to working remotely. People usually assume that switching to virtual work will be easy, but it is actually quite different from working in a traditional business setting. First, employees must smoothly adjust to the isolation of working remotely. In addition, communication styles, coworker interaction, and basic project management skills all need to be refined in order to be effective in a virtual environment. For example, employees must be much more direct and transparent in a virtual world in order to ensure all parts of a project are being completed—and on time.

For whole work groups making a transition to virtual work, it is important that some training be conducted together. Video chat works, but a better option is to get the team together in person to meet one another and gauge each other's personalities and skills. It may seem expensive, but the payoff for in-person training can be enormous, as there tends to be much less confusion and delay when communicating between team members. If in-person training is an option, employees should complete team bonding exercises (as discussed in Chapter 5) and learn about technology.

Technology training may seem a bit obvious, as employees should already know how to use their computers. However, Webcams, microphones, and online platforms, just to name a few, are a whole different ball game. Ignoring technology training can equate to lost productivity and, therefore, a loss of profitability. Simply giving out written instructions is not enough, as many people respond better to visual or hands-on instructions. In-person training is always the best choice for technology.

New Employees

New employees, especially those new to the workforce, have a decidedly easier time adapting to the virtual workplace. They do not have any old habits to unlearn and are not accustomed to their organization running a particular way. However, these employees actually require additional training when stepping into virtual roles. This extra training takes the place of the usual new-hire orientation.

Normally, a best practice is for new employees to attend a session with senior leadership to learn about the organization's strategy and mission and discuss the vision statement articulating where the company is headed, why it's headed in that direction, and why each employee is integral to the success of the organization. In addition, new employees would sit down with human resources to go over company policies and meet with various team members to learn about their different roles and responsibilities. Managers must come up with a whole new orientation system when training new virtual employees. Training with HR can be done over the phone as long as the employee is given a contact person for any questions that may arise. In addition, senior leadership can create a video to introduce the strategy and mission. However, I must emphasize again that in-person training is necessary for other job tasks. Through in-person training, new hires get a much better idea for the feel of the organization, as well as hands-on training, which allows for better comprehension and retention.

If in-person training is not possible, the best option is for managers to create training videos that walk new employees through each step of their responsibilities. Adding another sense to the training process (visual as well as aural) improves retention and comprehension. Employees should also be encouraged to take notes during video training to increase retention. Video training allows employees to train at their own pace, as well as go back and re-watch videos to clear up any confusion.

As training is completed, it is extremely important to track each employee's progress. A great way to do so is through a checklist of all necessary skills and processes employees must learn to effectively complete their job responsibilities. Managers should make sure that all of their direct reports are completing the necessary training to facilitate further advancement in their careers.

Employee Learning and Development

Learning and development programs have been some of the first to be widely available for remote training. The leading organizations in learning and development have already moved these programs to a virtual space, even for employees who do not work remotely. Virtual programs allow employees to choose which learning program they would like to take in order to fit their personal needs and goals. For example, some employees may need to brush up on their Microsoft Excel skills, whereas others may be more interested in improving general workplace skills such as communication. In addition, virtual programs allow employees to fit learning into their personal schedules.

For a virtual workforce, it is also a best practice to host a live learning and development event either annually or biannually. If it is not possible for all remote employees to attend this event, organizations should set up a live feed or video conference for employees to attend virtually. In addition to improving employees' skills and encouraging an increase in employee engagement, live training events also help build camaraderie and help employees feel like an integral and important part of the team.

To encourage ongoing learning and development, a best practice that I use with my direct reports is to touch base with employees every 30 days. I ask my employees to discuss what they have learned in the past 30 days, and what they would like to learn in the next 30 days. Through this process, I show my employees that I really care about their development and am willing to put in effort to see them succeed. In addition, by asking employees what they would like to learn rather than dictating the learning process, the employees gain buy-in into the process and are much more committed to success.

Finally, after training and development programs have been completed, a best practice is for managers to ask employees for feedback on training. This feedback can include what areas employees thought were the most useful, what areas could be improved, and anything they felt they should have learned about. Managers can then use this feedback to improve training and development programs in the future. In addition, the feedback will help managers determine whether employees have successfully transitioned into virtual roles or whether additional training, learning, and development is necessary.

MONITORING WORK AND EVALUATING PERFORMANCE

Monitoring virtual employees' work and providing guidance is quite different from checking in with employees who do not work remotely. You cannot simply stop by an employee's desk to make sure everything is on track, or notice when an employee seems to be panicking and step in to assist. As mentioned in Chapter 6, managers who check in too frequently with virtual employees will seem like micromanagers. In addition, these employees will feel as though their manager does not trust them to complete their work.

Monitoring virtual employees and their work is a key challenge for managers because they must find a balance between trusting employees to do their jobs and making sure employees perform up to par. Where virtual managers should really focus their efforts is on getting results. For instance, is the virtual employee consistently creating the outcomes desired by the virtual manager? Is the virtual employee reliably meeting deadlines? In order to create a results-based culture, managers can employ a number of techniques to monitor work and guide employees, such as status meetings and virtual tracking.

Status Meetings

As discussed in Chapter 6, regular status meetings are a great way to check in with employees without them feeling as though you are breathing down their necks. During these meetings, the employee should review his entire project list with the manager, and together they should discuss progress, any issues the employee is facing, and deadlines. These meetings are a great tool for virtual managers to gauge how employees feel about their workload and rearrange projects and deadlines as necessary. Status meetings also help both remote employees and their managers stay organized and ensure there are no issues.

As mentioned previously, some employees may prefer these meetings to take place less often—for example, weekly or biweekly—whereas other employees (especially Millennials) would like to have status meetings several times a week. The timing for status meetings should be determined on an employee-by-employee basis, and can be determined by employee preference. This type of meeting should be conducted live, either over the phone or via video chat.

For employees who work in different time zones from their managers, this type of meeting may not be possible without it becoming a regular nuisance to the virtual employee or the virtual manager. To ensure everyone stays in the loop, employees in this situation should send regular status updates via e-mail to their managers including all the information that would be conveyed in a status meeting. Alternately, their managers can set up a virtual tracking program to keep projects in check.

Virtual Tracking

Virtual tracking systems are a great option, either in place of or as a supplement to status meetings. There are many types of virtual trackers, from low-tech to high-tech. Low-tech trackers include shared documents, preferably spreadsheets, that the manager and all of her employees would be able to open and edit. This shared document can either be hosted on the organization's shared server or through a service like Google Documents. The tracker should contain all projects being worked on by all employees, the status of each project (including whether a project has been completed or is being edited), and the deadline. The document can be color-coded to show status—for example, green for projects that are currently in progress, red for missed deadlines, or yellow for immediate issues. The benefit of using this type of tracker is that it is very easy to create. However, low-tech trackers hosted on a shared server do have a drawback: Only one person is able to open the document and make updates at a time, which can become a large problem if there are a lot of people utilizing one document.

Another option is to create an Internet-based tracking system. This tracker could be hosted through the company's Intranet and would be able to be edited simultaneously by multiple users. In addition to the information mentioned previously, this type of system can include a number of other features to enhance organization. For example, users could set reminders to complete projects, comment on each other's projects, and send e-mails directly through the system. In addition, the virtual manager could use this system to track progress, as well as whether projects were completed accurately and on time. As well as helping managers understand their employees' individual workloads, tracking individual progress also works as a great motivator because it shows employees how they improve day-by-day. As Teresa Amabile, Harvard Business School professor, pointed out in her book, *The Progress Principle*, helping employees see the progress they make on a day-to-day basis is extremely important in keeping employees motivated and engaged in the workplace. The only issue with this type of system is that it takes quite a bit more effort to set up. However, online systems are much more robust, and therefore are well worth the time spent to create them.

Evaluating Virtual Workers vs. On-Site Employees

In some ways, evaluating the performance of remote employees is actually easier than evaluating on-site employees. Remote evaluations are very cut and dried. Because you do not see these employees in person on a regular basis, your opinion is less likely to be clouded by their behavior or any personal judgments you might make from physically seeing the employee. You just need to ask yourself: Did they perform, or didn't they?

In addition, due to the fact that most communication with remote employees is conducted electronically and that virtual managers are (hopefully!) also using virtual trackers, as discussed earlier, it is much easier for managers to take a look at what was completed, what type of instructions were given, and what errors took place when evaluating employees' performance. This availability of information allows managers to be much more objective when evaluating employees. Objectivity shows employees that evaluations are fair and balanced, rather than based on favoritism or personal, subjective feelings.

Something to consider when evaluating virtual employees is the quantity of work completed. Employees switching to virtual roles tend to not produce as much work during the first few months of working remotely. This drop-off is due to a change in routine and unfamiliarity with tasks and procedures. However, in time, these employees tend to become more productive than their in-office counterparts. They generally have fewer distractions and interruptions while working, and therefore can accomplish more than traditional employees. Keep these tendencies in mind when evaluating remote employees versus traditional employees. Employees who are new to working remotely should be considered similar to new hires and evaluated as such. Remote employees who have been in their positions for a considerable amount of time may actually have better performance than their on-site counterparts.

Informal vs. Formal Performance Reviews

It is important to give virtual employees as much feedback as possible due to the fact that they are not able to receive in-person cues about performance. Just like traditional employees, remote employees should have annual performance reviews. If possible, these reviews should be conducted in-person. If that is not possible, then video chat is the next best option. A best practice is for managers to evaluate employees, but also for employees to evaluate themselves in order to gauge employee perceptions of performance.

Annual performance reviews are a great way to connect with employees regarding their work, but, as with traditional employees, meeting annually is not enough. Despite everyone's best efforts, annual performance reviews still tend to focus on work completed most recently, rather than an entire year's worth of work. In addition, if there is a problem, managers need to discuss it with employees sooner rather than later to ensure changes are made and bad habits do not form. Informal performance reviews are a great way to provide this additional feedback. An informal performance discussion can occur as part of the regular check-ins virtual managers have with employees. During this time, the manager and employee can chat about any positive outcomes and behaviors, as well as any areas of opportunity for the employee. The manager should record anything discussed during these informal meetings so that all feedback can be incorporated in a fair and comprehensive way when it is time for the employee's formal performance review.

Performance Issues

One of the advantages uniquely afforded to virtual managers is that performance issues are more transparent and readily visible—underperforming virtual employees stick out like a sore thumb. Although this performance transparency is a benefit, it is *only* a benefit if it is acted upon and managed quickly. Clear signals of non-performance include missed goals, poor or nonexistent updates of progress or goal achievement, and non-participation in conference calls or Webinar meetings. Terrific virtual managers quickly pick up on these signals and act.

The way virtual managers respond to employee performance can determine the health and success of remote employee programs. By ensuring performance remains high, remote managers can optimize the productivity of their virtual team.

Monitoring Employees in the Field

Although the challenge of managing remote employees usually deals with internal issues, many managers face the challenge of managing employees who are interacting with customers in the field every day. In this virtual environment, employees must feel empowered to make decisions and act without manager input to quickly respond to customer issues. Managers of these employees need to help create this sense of empowerment by providing clear performance expectations and excellent training to their direct reports. In addition, a best practice is to check in regularly with the entire team through weekly report meetings to discuss what went right throughout the past week, what went wrong, and how the team's performance can be improved as a whole.

Case Study: Fairfax County Police Department

Managing virtual workers, specifically police officers, who spend the majority of their workday in the field, can be a daunting task. For 13 years, Mike A. McAlister, a former second lieutenant and sergeant at the Fairfax County Police Department in Virginia, directly supervised 12 to 15 police officers who were only in the station about 15 percent of the time. Despite the limited amount of in-person contact he had with his officers, McAlister always prided himself on empowering his employees to solve the problems they encountered in the field as they saw fit.

"I tried to engage and empower the officers by allowing them as much as possible within policy and procedure to solve their own problems," said McAlister.[3] "The more discretion and autonomy I permitted the officers to have, it allowed them to resolve issues on their own and learn from these experiences." With less supervision, the officers felt as if they had more ownership of how they worked and how they managed their calls.

If there was something his police officers wanted to change, McAlister would challenge them to find a solution and present it to him. "I would review the solution and troubleshoot it from a management perspective as I played devil's advocate," said McAlister. "If after my challenges it was appropriate, I would then present the proposal to the station captain and station lieutenant for their input and for them to forward it up the chain of command."

To engage and motivate the officers on his squad, McAlister regularly issued them challenges. "I would challenge their ability to solve an ongoing traffic issue or crime problem in our district," said McAlister. "I would let them come up with plans and methods for solving the issue. Then upon approval, they could act on their plan and work to solve the problem." By giving his officers an opportunity to come up with their own plans and methods for overcoming problems, McAlister increased their desire to tackle more issues without being prompted, and their engagement level rose as well.

McAlister monitored performance with the monthly, quarterly, and yearly statistical reports for cases handled, arrests, tickets, number of court cases presented by the officer, number of calls for service the officers responded to, and number of reports he or she wrote. He also reviewed citizen complaints and compliments. "I always tried to tie the training into areas where the officer was not performing at an acceptable level so the officer could improve," said McAlister.

For example, if an officer had difficulty writing complete and thorough reports containing all of the necessary information for a follow-up investigation by a detective, he might send that officer to a class on investigations so he (or she) would learn how follow-up investigations are performed and realize the critical need detectives have for a detailed preliminary police report. In contrast, for police officers who were performing well and were interested in a specific section or division in the police department, he would offer the officer training in that area or a temporary assignment within the section the officer wanted to work.

McAlister felt his toughest challenge was trying to motivate officers who were stuck in a rut and had been working in the same shift or police station for several years. "Typically, there was nothing new to their work and conditions. It was generally the same routine day after day and many of these officers had stopped challenging themselves," said McAlister. "Working with these officers to reignite the passion they displayed when they were younger was my biggest challenge." Regardless of the challenges he and his officers faced in the field, they effectively worked together to serve and protect their community.

Case Study: Fairfax County Fire and Rescue Department

From battling brush fires to quelling residential blazes, firefighters willingly put themselves in danger on a regular basis to help others. Lieutenant Marc Davidson, basic training compliance officer at the Fairfax County Fire and Rescue Academy, is a 16-year veteran of the department. Today, the department is one of the top 25 largest in the United States, approaching 1,400 uniformed and 370 civilian employees. Fairfax firefighters work 24-hour shifts where they are out in the field responding to calls approximately 15 to 25 percent of the day, depending on how busy their particular station is. Such a regimen requires frequent communication and strong leadership.

Clear and open communication is extremely important in a fire situation, especially when lives are on the line. "If I had to split a crew, we would communicate via radio," said Davidson.[4] "Once we are inside a structure fire, we have to stay within sight, touch, or hearing of each other. Visibility in the structure determines how we communicate." Whereas communication ensures Davidson and his firefighters remain connected, effective leadership enables firefighters to lead by example.

According to Davidson, leadership from the back, where a manager is simply telling employees to perform a task, typically does not work for his industry. As a result, leadership from the front, especially for a lieutenant, is essential for successfully managing a virtual team. "You always have to make sure your employees understand they are doing something you would do," said Davidson. "From mundane tasks to something more threatening, you have to make sure you are out in front and help them realize everything they do matters." Giving virtual workers an opportunity to propose a solution to a problem is also important. "I try not micromanage," said Davidson. "You have to make it a goal-oriented approach and give virtual workers a task and guidelines, allowing them to come up with a solution to the problem."

Because Davidson and his team often work in small units, they are able to closely monitor each other's actions and performance. After an incident, they always debrief to discuss what went right and what went wrong. "Administratively, I try to meet with [people] I am responsible for every three to six months," said Davidson. "Such meetings help my employees know where they are at, identify opportunities for improvement, and receive suggestions for growth."

Training and learning are ongoing in the department. When firefighters are not in the field, the rest of their time is devoted to preparing and training for calls. They regularly conduct drills inside and outside of the station. "Because of the nature of the job, training has to be a continuous process," said Davidson. "You can't sit back and take it easy. There is always something to learn about via PowerPoint presentations, articles, close-call reviews, and after-action reports."

> Because firefighters work in a high-risk, high-reward environment, most people assume they would want to be public recognized for their hard work. However, that is oftentimes not the case. "Most firefighters shy away from 'look at me' moments. They generally prefer low-key recognition," said Davidson. "Nonetheless, formal recognition (for example, a ribbon, an award, or a certificate of appreciation) is an important part of making sure your crew knows that they are valued, and should be considered whenever appropriate." For Davidson and other firefighters who put their lives on the line day after day, their greatest reward is their own awareness that they truly made a difference.

PAY: THE MYTHICAL DRIVER

You may have asked yourself why compensation was not included as one of the key drivers of engagement. The answer is simple: HR Solutions' Research Institute has actually found that increasing compensation has little impact on an employee's level of engagement. This is not to say pay is unimportant. Rather, it provides a different type of motivation to employees. Instead of being a reason people choose to stay with an organization or a reason they enjoy their work, pay is a reason to join or leave an organization.

When it comes to pay, virtual employees tend to respond in the same way as on-site employees. They are most likely to consider pay when applying for a job and/or considering accepting a job offer, and are most likely to accept a job offer if the compensation falls in the general range they were hoping to receive. In addition, throughout their tenure with an organization, virtual employees expect to receive pay raises based on performance and tenure. If employees start in a new job with a salary range lower than they expected to obtain, or if employees do not attain regular pay increases, they may feel dissatisfied with the job itself.

No matter whether employees work remotely or not, they are more likely to accept a pay cut if they are compensated otherwise—for example, with a better benefits package. The ability to work remotely is seen as a benefit by some employees, and therefore some will accept a pay cut in order to work remotely. In fact, 68 percent of employees who currently work on-site said they would be willing to work for less money if they were allowed to work remotely.[5] However, simply because employees are willing to work for less does not mean organizations should take advantage of that and "strategically" lower compensation packages. Instead, organizations operating under an extremely tight budget can use virtual work as a means of cutting back while still engaging their employees. However, this strategy should only be used as a short-term solution. Even if virtual employees may be willing to take a pay cut, they can still become dissatisfied due to pay if they feel the situation is unfair. Once these organizations are able to pay their employees more, they should increase compensation packages as soon as possible to avoid turnover and dissatisfaction. It is especially important to generously compensate top performers. These employees know what they are worth, and know they can receive that amount elsewhere.

The lion's share of compensation-related dissatisfaction stems from the communication of organizational compensation strategies (or lack thereof) and perceptions of fairness. A best practice is to create an organization-wide pay policy, and to keep pay levels the same whether an employee works on-site or remotely. To determine an organization's pay policy, look at annual pay increase statistics from the geographic area where employees are located. For example, organizations with employees located only in North America should use statistics from this continent, whereas organizations with employees spread out across the world should use global data. These statistics can help determine a range for pay increases, and should be included in any communication regarding the organization's pay policy.

An important note to make is that pay levels may not be equal across geographic areas due to changes in the cost of living. For example, an employee working in Iowa may earn less than a coworker in the same position living in New York City. Organizations should decide how salaries will vary according to cost of living for all employees and include this information in their policy.

Another consideration for organizations determining a pay policy for virtual employees is to incorporate the way salaries will change if an employee relocates, due to changes in the cost of living. For example, if an employee moves from Los Angeles to Wyoming, should her pay decrease? What if the employee moves from Wyoming to Los Angeles? A good policy is to base this decision on whether the organization transferred the employee, or if the employee moved voluntarily. Employees moving voluntarily would not receive a pay bump if moving to an area with a higher cost of living, whereas employees being transferred would receive this increase in salary. However, managers should reserve the right to increase salaries for high performers moving voluntarily. By helping high performers who move with cost-of-living increases, organizations decrease the chance that these employees will resign.

No matter what an organization decides to include in its pay policy, the strategy should be written down and communicated with employees. By clearly communicating this policy, employees can understand the organization's pay philosophy, see that their pay is fair, and ultimately be more satisfied with the pay they receive.

LEGAL IMPLICATIONS OF VIRTUAL WORKERS

As a manager or business owner, you are probably already familiar with various facets of employment law. However, you may not be aware of how a virtual work environment can present different risks for employers, simply through the nature of the work arrangement. This is not to say employing a virtual staff poses *more* risk than having on-site workers; in fact, I believe the opposite to be true. In today's quickly changing business world, you are likely undertaking a far greater risk by choosing *not* to employ virtual workers, simply through the missed opportunity of attracting and engaging top talent.

Phil Schreiber, partner at Holland & Knight in Chicago, has seen how virtual work policies affect employers. He firmly believes that by having the appropriate controls in place *before* any issues arise, common areas of the virtual work environment that cause legal hiccups can be easily managed. Schreiber's 14 years of experience representing employers and management in labor and employment law counseling and litigation have led to a deep understanding of what employers should be aware of when offering a virtual work policy. According to Schreiber, the following topics are a great place to start:

- Fairness in virtual privileges.
- Documenting disciplinary measures.
- Tracking hours and determining overtime.
- Monitoring computers.

Fairness in Virtual Privileges

When the option of working virtually is offered to employees as a privilege or benefit, fairness comes to the forefront of legal issues. Although offering the option to work remotely to those who have earned it is often a very successful strategy, it is important to have an objective way of determining which employees receive this benefit. When managers subjectively decide which employees can work remotely without internal guidelines, they are exposing themselves to the risk of discrimination claims. Employers can safeguard themselves by having a detailed policy in place that determines which employees are eligible for virtual work. Managers should also keep records of how employees meet or do not meet those requirements.

It is worth noting that bending the rules for certain employees based on their personal situations can be a nice thing to do, but other employees may perceive it as favoritism or a bias in the policy. For example, allowing employees recovering from a health problem to work at home but denying new mothers the same privilege may be viewed as discrimination against new mothers, and in violation of the Pregnancy Discrimination Act. Schreiber says that employees may or may not raise an issue with this policy, but if they did, they would have some legal standing regarding unfair special treatment by your organization.

Documenting Disciplinary Measures

A very common pitfall in employing virtual workers relates to the complications of disciplinary action and the separation process. Oftentimes, it simply takes managers longer to determine when a virtual worker is not performing up to the proper standards. As stressed earlier, trusting virtual workers and resisting the urge to micromanage is important for engagement. Additionally, monitoring actions is generally more difficult when one is not face-to-face with employees. Unfortunately, this combination of circumstances can create a situation in which virtual employees get away with unacceptable behavior much longer than on-site employees probably would.

When a virtual manager learns that a direct report has been pulling the wool over his eyes, there is the inclination to feel betrayed and respond out of anger. This reaction can create legal issues if the reasons for disciplinary action have not been properly documented, or if the communication to the employee is unprofessional or inappropriate.

The communication method—how the message is delivered—often plays a role as well. When managers address behavioral issues with on-site employees, immediately speaking in person is often the preferred method because the issue is of a serious nature. In a professional setting, face-to-face meetings are often most effective when addressing conflict because we have a natural tendency to tone down our emotions and watch what we say. With the person staring right back at you, it is easier to remember we are all human, and all humans make mistakes, which will keep communication respectful and professional. However, when employees are virtual, managers often turn to e-mail instead of meeting in person, and there is something about written communication that can make people forget about how their message will be perceived. Because they do not have to see the recipient's reaction upon receiving the message, people are often less concerned about how it comes across, and they use stronger words and a more confrontational tone than they would have in an in-person meeting. It's like firing words into a black hole; people assume they will not have to think about those words after they hit the *Send* button.

This reaction by virtual managers is exactly what frequently causes legal issues down the road. When confronting someone via e-mail, those words will always be there in black and white. If an employee feels her manager's reaction was inappropriate, there is written proof of what was said in the heat of the moment. If the conflict leads to a lawsuit, conversations can easily be manipulated in court. According to Schreiber, when snippets of an exchange are taken out of context and flashed in front of a jury, any unfortunate choices in words or tone can come across as evidence of unfair treatment or discrimination. "This is the type of information that really resonates with a jury," says Schreiber.[6] Of course, managers should always make an effort to rise above emotional reactions from workplace occurrences, but this is especially important in e-mail communication. By taking a step back and thinking about how to communicate with virtual employees *before* taking action, virtual managers will be in a better mindset to deliver an appropriate message.

When it comes to documenting the disciplinary path for virtual employees, appropriate communication encompasses a few different aspects:

- You must have proof that the issue that required disciplinary action was addressed. The offense should be clearly stated to explain exactly why disciplinary action is taking place and what behavior or performance standards are expected going forward.

- All repercussions should be mentioned, including discharge.
- Any applicable written policies should be cited or quoted.
- A third party should be able to read your message without sensing underlying sarcasm, anger, or snootiness. Tone *does* matter. If you are unsure whether your message is appropriate, it is a good idea to run it past someone in Human Resources. Explaining your way out of something is a lot more difficult than avoiding actions that need to be explained.

Tracking Hours and Determining Overtime

Tracking hours for nonexempt employees (in other words, employees entitled by law to overtime pay) can be more difficult in the virtual environment. On-site employees are often visible to their manager when they come and go, or they have to punch in and out. When employees are remote, it is harder to track their schedule with the same certainty. If employees work remotely from computers, it should be possible to track the times they are logged into the system, but if virtual workers are in the field with clients or customers, organizations might have to get more creative with tracking hours. Depending on the work situation, employers should have effective and auditable measures in place to ensure that virtual workers are accurately recording their hours.

Employers also must determine if and when overtime is appropriate or required for nonexempt virtual workers. Are employees on the clock when they are traveling to and from meetings? What about unforeseen situations, such as an unexpected layover or if a client cancels when an employee is already en route to meet with him? These situations can cause confusion on behalf of the employer and employee in calculating overtime and compensation. If there isn't a policy outlining detailed guidelines for determining what constitutes hours worked for determining overtime pay, employers are at a high risk of wage and hour litigation.

Monitoring Computers

Some people think monitoring virtual activity is primarily done to ensure that employees are working, but there is a far greater reason why organizations put in the time and effort: Because one person's actions could be detrimental to the entire organization, through sharing internal information or false communication, employers have the responsibility to monitor the virtual communication and Internet activity of staff members.

Most organizations have a policy employees must agree to and sign that removes their expectations of privacy while using company machines, networks, and servers. However, Schreiber says this agreement can be become complicated for employees who work from home: "When employees work remotely on their own devices, the line between work and personal use can become blurred, causing discrepancy in privacy expectations."[7] Regardless of the work situation, employers must create a privacy policy to monitor virtual communication when employees are remote. It is essential for privacy policies to be abundantly clear. Perhaps the policy states the employer is able to monitor virtual communication between 9 a.m. and 5 p.m., certain folders on the hard drive, or only when logged in to the company server. Whatever the organization determines appropriate must be spelled out for the employee, and compliance should be recorded.

Although there are aspects of the virtual environment that can cause interesting legal situations, most are avoidable by simply being aware of the risks. In addition to the aforementioned points, there are numerous state law issues that come into play when working with virtual employees, such as unemployment coverage, workers' compensation coverage, wage and hour laws, and fair employment practices. For complete legal advice on employing virtual workers, nothing is more valuable than a knowledgeable and experienced employment law attorney.

BALANCING GROUND RULES AND FLEXIBILITY

Organizations looking to create or hire a virtual workforce tend to first craft a number of ground rules to keep employees in check, ranging from practical to nonsensical. The thought process is: "I can't see these employees. If I don't have firm rules in place, how will I know they're working?" These organizations often institute excessive rules that do nothing to build engagement, help employees, or contribute positively to the business. Don't get me wrong: Setting ground rules for remote employees is very important. In fact, many employees want rules so that they understand expectations. According to HR Solutions' Research Institute, only 68 percent of employees believe organizational policies have been clearly communicated at their organization. However, virtual managers should be wary of creating rules for the sake of creating rules. Instead, ground rules should focus on making the virtual workplace as productive and efficient as possible.

Working Hours

One of the most common rules established by organizations with a virtual workforce is to set designated work hours. This rule typically defines when remote employees should be at their work stations and reachable by phone or e-mail. However, if one of the main employee benefits of having a virtual workforce is to increase flexibility, then rules about required working hours may not make sense for an organization. Unless there is a specific reason why employees should have required start and end times for their day (for example, the employee is paid by the hour or the employee works directly with customers or clients), then this type of rule is likely unnecessary. If an employee's job function is to serve customers, then her customers' needs will probably dictate the hours she works. However, if employees who do not work directly with customers are most productive in the evening, then why not allow them to work later in the day, and vice versa? Accommodating virtual employees' peak work times will not only establish a culture of flexibility, but will also ultimately create better outcomes for the business because employees will be producing better work while on the clock.

Another challenge for organizations is tracking the number of hours worked by virtual employees. If traditional employees within the organization are required to work a certain number of hours per week, then, for the sake of fairness, remote employees should have similar rules in place. However, we may see more results-oriented workplaces in the future, rather than the traditional time-oriented workday. Results-oriented workplaces focus on the work that is completed and the results that are produced by employees, rather than the number of hours worked per week.

Pilot results-oriented programs conducted by companies such as Best Buy have produced very positive results, in which employees are shown to actually be more productive and more engaged when they do not have required working hours. At Best Buy's corporate office, employees have no required start times, have no required weekly hours, and are allowed to work from any location they choose. Their HR department first initiated a program they called ROWE (Results-Only Work Environment) in 2003, and it was adopted company-wide in 2007. Since starting the program, pilot departments have seen a dramatic change in productivity and employee retention. In fact, organizations following the ROWE program typically see an average 35-percent improvement in productivity among their workforce, as well as a 90-percent reduction in turnover.[8]

For virtual employees, my recommendation is to follow the results-oriented theory. As long as employees complete their work on time and quality remains high, they can be allowed to work whatever number of hours a week they prefer. This change to a results-oriented approach puts a focus on performance and encourages work-life balance. In most cases, employees will manage their time more wisely when they know management isn't expecting them to be at work for a set period of time.

Some employees may work fewer hours, but many are likely to actually work more hours in results-oriented workplaces because they care about producing the best-quality work they can. My brother-in-law, Dan, works from home 90 percent of the time. He pointed out that without time restrictions, organizations actually may get a better deal from employees. For example, virtual employees are likely to roll out of bed and start working right away, as well as continue checking e-mail until they go to bed. Dan actually puts in more hours when working from home than he does when in the office.

Remote managers following a results-oriented policy should set ground rules from the beginning regarding job performance. These rules should state that if performance becomes an issue, employees will have to go back to having a required number of hours per week and/or required start and end times for the day.

The idea of throwing out office hours completely may scare some virtual managers. As mentioned in Chapter 2, managers must let go, and learn to trust their employees. If they cannot trust their employees to actually complete the work assigned to them, then the virtual manager may have made the wrong hire at the start.

To help remote employees and managers work together efficiently, a good alternative to a results-oriented workplace is to have general hours when the entire team should be working. For example, at HR Solutions, we have a floating start time: Employees can arrive at the office any time between 7 and 9 o'clock in the morning, and leave after working an eight-hour day. Through this policy, *all* employees should be at work between 9 a.m. and 3 p.m. In virtual workplaces, managers may choose to have fewer overlapping hours to provide flexibility and aid employees working from different time zones. For example, required office hours could be between 10 a.m. and 3 p.m. That way, virtual managers and employees are able to contact one another throughout the day and remain productive.

Response Time

For employees working remotely, especially those without specific working hours, there should be a clear policy regarding the desired response time to both internal and external requests. A good rule of thumb is to give employees three business hours to respond to external requests and one business day to respond to any e-mail or voice-mail inquiries from internal employees. If the employee is not able to fulfill a request made in a voice mail or e-mail in that business day, then he or she should at least acknowledge receipt of the message and give a time line for completion. By establishing a common standard, employees will not only know the amount of time they have to respond, but will also feel as though they do not have to be constantly plugged in: If a request comes in at night, the employee should not feel as though he must respond immediately. Just because an employee works remotely does not mean she should always be working!

Workspace Requirements

Another rule many organizations put into place is that remote employees must have a dedicated workspace they will use every day. Once again, this type of rule hinders flexibility, as some employees may want to work from a coffee shop, the neighborhood park, or a vacation home. As long as they have an Internet connection and telephone, employees can really be allowed to work from anywhere. An exception, of course, should be made for meetings, which should take place in a private area, for both noise control and confidentiality. In addition, employees working with sensitive information, such as social security numbers, should be careful about the workspace they choose, for security reasons.

Another great best practice is to require employees to travel to the organization's main office. The frequency of visits can be determined by the distance the employee lives from the organization. For example, an employee who lives nearby could be required to come in once per week, whereas other employees may be required to make the trip once per month, once per quarter, or once per year.

Dress Code

Believe it or not, some organizations actually establish dress codes for virtual employees—"Employees should not wear pajamas while working," for example. The purpose of creating a dress code for remote workers is to ensure they are in a professional mindset during working hours. Rules such as this tend to be overbearing and unnecessary, especially if there is no way to check whether employees are actually following them. However, an exception should be made for meetings conducted via video chat. For internal meetings, the dress code should be the same as for on-site employees who will join the call. That way, on-site employees won't log in wearing suits and ties while virtual employees show up in a robe and slippers, which will prevent any perceived unfairness. In addition, for external meetings with clients, organizations may want to set a more formal dress code, such as business casual or business formal.

Meeting Etiquette

Laying down ground rules for all virtual meetings will save a lot of future headaches. A leader should be appointed for each meeting to direct conversations and make sure everyone stays on track according to a set agenda. The agenda should be sent to all meeting attendees prior to the meeting so they can prepare any comments or questions they will want to share. In live meetings, employees often use visual cues to determine who will speak next and whether someone needs to interject a comment. For meetings taking place over the phone, the meeting leader should act as a moderator and guide the conversation so the virtual meeting runs smoothly.

Another standard rule is to ask employees not to do anything else while attending the virtual meeting—no answering e-mails or instant messaging, no playing with their dog, and no eating. In essence, they should behave as they would during an in-person meeting. By cutting out background tasks, employees will improve their listening abilities, comprehension, and retention, thereby making remote meetings more productive.

It is often harder in general for people to pay attention during phone conversations than when speaking in person. In addition, it is easier for employees to get away with directing their attention elsewhere during virtual meetings. To keep employees focused, the meeting moderator can periodically ask if anyone else has any comments or would like to add to the conversation, and specifically ask the opinions of any non-contributors.

Team Roles

To ensure that virtual teams work effectively together, remote managers must create clear guidelines establishing each team member's role, including that of the team manager. How can you easily and most effectively clarify roles and responsibilities? Simply create a roles and responsibilities list and distribute it to all of your direct reports. After employees have received the list, ask them individually for their input. Additionally, managers should ask team members for any preferences they may have regarding job content. Before asking for feedback, you might be wise to set expectations by making it clear that no job on earth is composed of 100 percent of the tasks and duties the job incumbent fancies doing. All of the "have to" and not-so-exciting tasks cannot be conveniently handed off to other team members.

By the way, a tangential but important benefit of asking your remote workers for feedback on this summary sheet is that you are getting their buy-in to the plan up-front. The value of garnering this buy-in is monumental down the road when it is time for the employee to fulfill her promise to execute her roles and responsibilities. This tactfully political and strategic step will eliminate myriad virtual headaches and roadblocks later on.

Once you have fielded the feedback, compare it to your own original mapping of the team's roles and responsibilities as you initially envisioned them. Make the natural adjustments and then ask for more feedback on that draft of what now amounts to the team's charter. Once this document is completed, put it into action for testing purposes. After 30 days, assess and recalibrate the plan if necessary.

Success is not final, failure is not fatal: it is the courage to continue that counts.

—Winston Churchill

Formalizing Ground Rules

No matter what rules your organization ultimately decides to set for virtual employees, make sure the expectations for remote work are clearly stated and documented. These rules and regulations should be distributed to all remote employees, who should be required to sign and return a copy, which should be kept in each employee's personnel file. By setting common standards, you ensure buy-in from employees and gain confidence that everyone understands their expectations from day one. If a problem should arise, you can always return to these documents to show employees the conditions they agreed to follow when working remotely.

TRANSITIONING EMPLOYEES OUT OF A VIRTUAL ENVIRONMENT

Some people simply cannot be effective outside of the workplace.

Imagine you've recently given a team member the opportunity to work remotely, but unfortunately he is not succeeding as a virtual employee. He does not complete work on time, or respond to internal or external inquiries in a timely manner. The quality of his work is suffering, and his clients are not as satisfied with their interactions with him as they previously were. You know he has great potential, and you know he's not completely disengaged from the organization; he just isn't cut out for virtual work.

Understand Why

As a top-notch virtual manager, you must first understand exactly why the employee is not succeeding virtually. You should already have an open and honest relationship established with the remote worker, given the importance of communication when working virtually. Before making any changes to the employee's working relationship, you should initiate a conversation to fully grasp why the team member is struggling while working at a distance. Ask the employee questions to better educate yourself regarding the individual's current engagement level, relative both to the organization and to her work. Encourage the employee to outline in detail any difficulties she is having. Perhaps she is not responding to voice mails and e-mails because she is not receiving them due to technological issues. Maybe the employee has become ambivalent because she is not being recognized appropriately, she feels her career growth opportunities are stagnant, or she is not receiving enough support from management or coworkers to complete her job duties. If the reason the remote team member is not thriving virtually is fixable, put an action plan in motion and set a time line to gauge improvement.

Communicate the "Why" Behind the Change

As always, communication and open dialogue are the keys to a successful transition from virtual work back to an on-site work status. Too many managers make the mistake of simply notifying the employee of the change, but not explaining the "why." People are only human, and therefore they want to be able to ask questions about changes that will alter their work dynamic. Seize this opportunity to alleviate any ambiguity the employee may have, allowing the individual to re-engage and re-energize in his office role. Do not present the transition as a punishment, but rather unveil it as a valuable move to everyone involved. Employees want to be empowered to make a difference and contribute to the organization, so it is important to stress the greater contribution the employee can make by working in the head office or at another business site. When the transition is positioned in this positive fashion, employees will be more willing to embrace the change to the physical office.

In addition to the virtual employee, on-site employees will also wonder how they will be affected by the addition of a new team member. Hence, there is a strong need for communication not only to the transitioning employee, but also with those who will welcome the employee. Over-communication is necessary to ensure everyone understands what will occur during the transition and why the transition is happening in the first place. Anticipate any challenges you may face, and be proactive in working with employees to make the transition as easy as possible.

Establish a Transition Plan

Once the decision has been made to transition a virtual employee and he has been notified, the communication to the internal staff should include a time line for when the transition will occur. Bringing employees back into the on-site world will not necessarily occur quickly or easily. Data files and computer programs need to be transferred, supplies need to be purchased, and space needs to be designated. Creating a detailed plan outlining exactly what needs to be completed prior to the transition will make for a seamless change. A detailed time line will also allow the remote worker to prepare himself for the change, making it smoother for everyone involved.

Transition Challenges

One challenge employees will face during the transition involves interactions with coworkers. If the virtual employee was working on site prior to becoming a virtual worker, she will need to reestablish connections with her coworkers; if the employee has always worked at a distance, he will likely need to establish entirely new connections. Effective virtual managers should recognize the importance of coworker relationships regarding retention, and exert extra effort to establish bonds between the virtual employee and on-site team members, enabling the transitioned individual to build a strong support system.

Virtual employees also face the challenge of becoming accustomed to new protocols and procedures. Different locations across an organization may have foreign methods for accomplishing tasks, different ways of communicating, or simply other technology with which the remote worker is unfamiliar. For example, imagine you have always used a PC, but in the office work environment, only Macs are available. This technological change would definitely take some adjustment before you would feel familiar with the functionalities of the new computer.

Employees who are already working on-site can help get the virtual employee acquainted with the physical office space. Additionally, virtual managers should be available to answer any questions the virtual employee may have throughout the transition period.

On-Boarding the Virtual Employee

Remote supervisors should treat the employee's first day in the physical office almost as though she is a new member of the team. After all, in a way she is. Similar to new hires, virtual employees may be unfamiliar with the culture of a particular locale. They are meeting people they often have never personally met before. They are not necessarily aware of the chain of command, and they probably will not know their way around the office. Adapting best practices for on-boarding new employees will be beneficial to their incorporation into the on-site office and increase the chances they will be actively engaged.

Make the first day on-site a celebration. Celebrate the contributions the virtual employee has already made to the organization, and showcase how his contributions will be even greater in the physical office. Introduce him to the entire team to foster coworker relations, and make him feel comfortable. Provide the appropriate keys, supplies, and office space so the employee feels there really is a spot for him within the organization. It's amazing how something as simple as providing a space in which to work will increase feelings of inclusion among employees. Encourage on-site team members to proactively interact with the remote worker as well. Organize a teambuilding event, such as a team lunch or meeting, to make the employee feel part of the on-site culture.

Preempting Disengagement

A key element in the transition from virtual employee to on-site employee is increasing or maintaining the employee's engagement with the organization. Meet regularly with the transitioned employee to ensure the change is going smoothly and the employee is comfortable in her new position. During these meetings, discuss the employee's engagement level and her particular drivers and detractors for engagement.

It is important to redefine and emphasize the employee's role within the organization to alleviate any engagement detractors. When team members are pulled from working at a distance, they may feel they failed the organization, and thus are inadequate and not cut out for their job responsibilities. Virtual managers must stress that this is not the case (because you have already determined the employee is capable of the job's performance expectations). You should emphasize that the remote worker *is* a good fit for the organization, just not when working at a distance.

Remote supervisors must work closely with the employee to ensure he understands they want him as part of the team, that he is an asset, and that he is contributing to the organization's overall success.

When employees are removed from the virtual workforce, they may also feel they are no longer trusted by management, which can result in decreased engagement. Because trust is vital to a successful working relationship, leadership must do everything in its power to make employees feel trusted despite the loss of virtual privileges. Provide employees with autonomy in other ways to assure them you have not lost faith in their abilities and you trust them to be successful in their jobs. Give them responsibilities and allow them to follow through on projects with minimal supervision. Do not constantly micromanage the employee, as constant scrutiny will hinder the development of trust, especially because the employee is used to simply being evaluated on the final deliverable produced, rather than her progress along the way. Despite no longer working virtually, employees should still be trusted to do their work as long as performance is meeting expectations.

As you can see from the aforementioned examples, an employee who is transitioned out of the virtual environment is likely to be ambivalent or disengaged. If the employee enters the office setting ambivalent, there is a chance to re-engage her in the organization despite removing her from the virtual world. Utilize the key drivers of engagement to cultivate a connection with the organization. On day one at the physical office, encourage and facilitate interactions between the virtual employee and actively engaged employees to reinvigorate engagement. If the employee is disengaged, however, it will be difficult to help him form a connection with the organization. When moving disengaged employees, you should consider transitioning them out of the organization entirely as they often have a tendency to infect others with their negativity, leading to a spiral effect of disengagement within the organizational culture.

What about an employee who has been working remotely from the other side of the world? This transition may not be nearly as simple, as relocation costs and other personal obligations that hinder relocation must be considered. Give the employee the opportunity to discuss his feelings about the proposed situation with you. If management and the employee do not agree on the best way to handle the change, it may be futile to expect the transition to be successful. At this point, the virtual manager should consider parting ways with the employee.

All in all, an unsuccessful virtual employee is *not* a lost cause. Management must simply make a change in order to enable employees to reach their maximum potential. Utilizing the aforementioned best practices will allow for a seamless transition from the remote world to the on-site office.

FINAL THOUGHTS

THE ULTIMATE VIRTUAL ENVIRONMENT: SPACE

When most people think about working remotely, we envision a quiet home office, a coffee shop, or a perhaps a client's headquarters. For Jerry Linenger, retired United States Navy flight surgeon and NASA astronaut, "working virtually" has a whole different meaning.

Linenger always wanted to be an astronaut. When he first got the call in 1992 that NASA wanted him to enter the space program and train to become an astronaut, he threw the phone up in the air, and started jumping up and down and screaming with excitement. He was in for an adventure the likes of which most of us only dream.

Throughout the next several years, Linenger went on to spend nearly five months in space, logging 50 million miles—the equivalent distance of more than 110 trips to and from the moon. One of the missions he took part in aboard the Russian Space Station *Mir* ended up being one of the most dangerous and dramatic missions in space history. Faced with countless challenges and unexpected situations, Linenger is an expert in the virtual work environment. His experiences working in outer space have enabled him to give advice that is certainly applicable to those of us with our feet on the ground.

Photo of Jerry Linenger, courtesy of NASA.

Proper Training

Astronauts are nothing if not over-prepared, and this is a primary reason why they have been able to achieve remarkable successes at such a great distance. Specific training measures vary depending on an astronaut's specialty, but all astronauts go through an intense program in which they train for myriad situations and practice the same skills hundreds and hundreds of times, some for several years, before ever going to space. "Bottom line," said Linenger, "when on your own, you must over-train on all tasks. You must know the procedures cold."[1] As Linenger points out, properly completing routine tasks can be a matter of life and death. For example, if an astronaut moves the wrong oxygen pressurization flow valve on his or her spacesuit, there is the risk of running out of oxygen midway through the task. In other situations, one wrong move can compromise the whole mission, such as in completing experiments where there is no room for error. "You are performing high-stakes tasks day after day. It's a *one chance to get it right* experiment," said Linenger.

Final Thoughts

Considering the importance of astronauts' duties while they are in space, training has been the best way to prepare them for success. Organizations in all industries are wise to follow this example. A good measure for determining an employee's competency in his tasks is to see if he can complete them when outside support isn't readily available. When employees understand how to do their assignments without help from managers or coworkers, managers know their employees can be successful virtually. Even if job duties at your organization aren't as critical as those in space travel, productivity and quality are still measures for success.

Proper Tools

When Linenger was onboard the *Mir*, there were parts of the space craft that were 13 years old, even though the design life of these parts was only three years. Essentially, the tools and resources the crew had access to were in many ways subpar, and there were numerous instances when this almost caused a catastrophe. "We had breakdowns pretty much on a daily basis," recalls Linenger. He experienced a raging fire on the spacecraft, failure of the oxygen supply systems, and failure of the carbon dioxide scrubbing system. As if that weren't enough action for an entire lifetime, a computer failure caused the crew to topple through space completely uncontrolled. "Talk about a scary moment," said Linenger, remembering the emergency. "[Being on the] dark side of the Earth, tumbling though space...the blackness and silence unnerve you."

The biggest setbacks Linenger and other crew members endured on their mission were the result of faulty tools and equipment. Even though these professionals had the training and experience to be successful, they were almost cut short by their lack of adequate resources.

An equipment failure that can cause employees to plummet into nothingness is, without a doubt, the ultimate virtual catastrophe. Although the consequences are a little different here on Earth, providing and maintaining proper equipment is nevertheless non-negotiable. When employees are not able to do their jobs effectively because they do not have the proper resources, it is poor management, plain and simple.

Fostering Communication

Linenger's time on *Mir* was actually pretty quiet—in the sense that there wasn't much talking. He was in space for five months with two Russian cosmonauts who spoke no English, but despite the language barrier, the crew was able to collaborate and accomplish their goals. This is no small miracle, especially considering that their communication satellite broke during the journey, which was their only means of receiving guidance and instruction from Earth. To make matters worse, due to economic constraints, Mission Control–Moscow was only able to keep one ground communication station working, instead of the recommended series of communication stations around the world (another detrimental effect stemming from a lack of resources). As a result, the crew was lucky if they were able to communicate with Earth once every 90 minutes, and only for a few minutes at best.

These conditions certainly hindered the ability to communicate, showing that, first and foremost, having the right virtual communication tools is the foundation for good communication. If you think of Linenger's communication experience on *Mir* the next time you drop a call, hopefully it will help you put your challenges in perspective.

In addition to proper communication tools, virtual employees and managers must work together to proactively share information and understand one another. "Err on the side of sending too much information," Linenger advises managers. "It is uncomfortable [for employees] to ask for help. You have pride. You have worked hard to prepare yourself to do autonomous work. You do not want the people...to judge you as incompetent."

Managers should anticipate this common employee perception and proactively offer as much support as is possible. Linenger says managers should always ask their virtual workers how they can be helpful to them. In addition, managers should never judge their employees harshly, especially when they might not fully understand what they are going through. If open, secure, and trusted communication is not established, the virtual worker will tend to be even less willing to ask for guidance. She will be stuck performing at a level that is not internally rewarding and does not advance the organization to the optimum level. Instead, by encouraging open communication, trust will be fostered.

Feedback and Recognition

Many people consider astronauts to be the ultimate knowledge workers. After all, it is one of the most exclusive career paths with the smallest number of job openings in the entire world. The people who are accepted into space programs are the absolute best of the best, so it is easy to assume astronauts probably know more about their job duties than their colleagues who are helping them from the ground. With this in mind, you might be surprised to know astronauts desire constructive feedback and recognition just like other professionals. "Working autonomously with little feedback is tough," said Linenger. "You find yourself doubting your own abilities. Even a well-trained astronaut feels much more insecure than you might imagine when cut off from mankind, colleagues and trainers for months at a time. You crave some refresher training or tips on how to improve, and how to be even more successful in accomplishing the mission's goals."

Virtual managers should keep this in mind. If Linenger—a Naval Academy graduate, who holds duel masters degrees in policy and systems management, doctorates in both medicine and research methodology, and three honorary doctorate degrees in science—can sometimes feel the need for extra feedback and instruction, so does John Doe in outside sales.

In addition to constructive feedback, praise and recognition are essential in the virtual environment. Employees are universally motivated through their manager's and organization's appreciation for a job well done. "You crave some recognition for the tasks accomplished," said Linenger. "At the end of the day, strapping myself inverted on a wall to sleep, the sense of accomplishment is what allowed a good night's sleep."

Virtual managers should go out of their way to provide feedback and encouragement on performance on a regular basis. Sharing insight and tips on performance is especially important for distance workers, as they desire a deeper understanding of whether they are meeting expectations from so far away.

SUMMARY

Oftentimes, managing a virtual workforce can seem like a daunting task. There are so many elements that cause uncertainty, that virtual managers frequently have a tendency to take on added and unnecessary stress. Considering Linenger's experience of working in a virtual environment certainly puts our challenges into perspective; although we may worry about our direct reports having the knowledge they need to survive in the virtual environment, we can take comfort in knowing they are not quite so far away.

It is important for employers and virtual managers to take a step back and look at the big picture. Workplace hiccups can occur in any environment. Whereas a mishap may seem like a mountain when it is taking place, it will likely look like a molehill a month down the road. In essence, when a challenging situation arises from a remote work arrangement, it isn't time to throw in the towel. It's time to rise to the occasion.

NOTES

*All Websites were accessed September 9–14, 2011.

CHAPTER 1

1. "Statistics," Telework Research Network, *www.teleworkresearchnetwork.com/telecommuting-statistics*.
2. Ibid.
3. Robert Half International and CareerBuilder.com, "Executive Summary: A Tale of Two Job Markets," *The EDGE Report*, September 2008, *www.rhi.com/External_Sites/downloads/RHI/PressReleases/EDGE_Report_08-2008.pdf*.
4. Rieva Lesonsky, "Telecommuting Makes Employees More Productive: Survey Says," *The Huffington Post*, August 13, 2011, *www.huffingtonpost.com/2011/08/13/telecommuting-employees-productivity_n_926285.html*.
5. Amelia Forczak, "Working From Home: Benefits for the Employer," HR Solutions eNews, March 2011, *www.hrsolutionsinc.com/enews_0311/Working_From_Home_0311.html*.
6. Dana E. Friedman, "Workplace Flexibility: A Guide for Companies," Families and Work Institute, *www.familiesandwork.org/3w/tips/downloads/companies.pdf*.

7. Ted Samson, "Research: Telecommuters with Flex Time Can Handle 50 Percent More Work," InfoWorld, June 3, 2010, *www.infoworld.com/d/green-it/research-telecommuters-flex-time-can-handle-50-percent-more-work-866*.

8. Ed Frauenheim, "Commute Stress Out of Control?," CNET News, December 1, 2004, *http://news.cnet.com/Commute-stress-out-of-control/2100-1022_3-5473133.html*.

9. Kristin Smith and Reagan Baughman, "Caring for America's Aging Population: A Profile of the Direct-Care Workforce," *Monthly Labor Review*, September 2007, 20–26, *www.bls.gov/opub/mlr/2007/09/art3full.pdf*.

10. GreenBiz Staff, "Flex-Time Workers Add Two Days to Their Workweek," GreenBiz.com, June 4, 2010, *www.greenbiz.com/news/2010/06/04flex-time-workers-add-two-days-their-workweek*.

11. "Pros and Cons," Telework Research Network, *www.teleworkresearchnetwork.com/pros-cons*.

12. "Telecommuting Facts," United States Department of Agriculture, Farm Service Agency, *www.fsa.usda.gov/FSA/hrdapp?area=home&subject=wpsv&topic=tel-tf*.

13. "Cost-Benefits," InnoVisions Canada, *www.ivc.ca/costbenefits.htm*.

14. Kate Lister and Tom Harnish, "The State of Telework in the U.S.," Telework Research Network, June 2011, *www.workshifting.com/downloads/downloads/Telework-Trends-US.pdf*.

15. "Telework Tax Incentives and Reimbursements," SuiteCommute, April 2009, *www.suitecommute.com/about-2/monthly-newsletters/apr-tax-incentives/*.

16. Microsoft Office, "Microsoft Home Office Makeover," Microsoft Office Fact Sheet, June 2007, *www.microsoft.com/presspass/presskits/2007office/docs/MSHomeOfficeFS.doc*.

17. Jonathan Spira and Joshua Feintuch, "The Cost of Not Paying Attention: How Interruptions Impact Knowledge Worker Productivity," Basex, Inc., 2005, *www.workshifting.com/downloads/downloads/Workshifting%20Benefits-The%20Bottom%20Line.pdf*.

18. Kate Lister, "Workshifting Benefits: The Bottom Line," Telework Research Network, May 2010, *www.workshifting.com/downloads/downloads/Workshifting%20Benefits-The%20Bottom%20Line.pdf*.

19. Alexandra Guadagno, "Working Smart: 3 Tips to Accomplish Much More in Less Time," Human Resources IQ, June 13, 2011, *www.humanresourcesiq.com/effective-management-toolkit/articles/working-smart-3-tips-to-accomplish-much-more-in-mu/&mac=HRIQ_OI_Featured_2011&utm_source=humanresourcesiq.com&utm_medium=email&utm_campaign=HrOptIn&utm_content=6/15/11*.

20. U.S. GSA Recommendations to Assist Cost Recovery/ROI Strategies and Budget Planning, May 2006 (attributed to WorldatWork, "Exploring Telework as a Business Continuity Strategy," 2005); Non-telecommuting average of 2.4% (5.8 days) per year CCH 17th Annual Unscheduled Absence Survey, *www.workshifting.com/downloads/downloads/Workshifting%20Benefits-The%20Bottom%20Line.pdf*.

21. "Absenteeism," SuiteCommute, *www.suitecommute.com/research-and-statistics/statistics/absenteeism/*.

22. Leslie Bonacum, "CCH Survey Finds Most Employees Call in "Sick" for Reasons Other Than Illness," CCH, October 10, 2007, *www.cch.com/press/news/2007/20071010h.asp*.

CHAPTER 2

1. Charles Bullock and Jennifer Tucker Klein, "Virtual Work Environments in the Post-Recession Era," Brandman University, 2011, *www.brandman.edu/pdf/virtual_teams_brandman_forrester_white_paper.pdf*.

2. Virtualteambuilders, "Employee Engagement—You Can't Do it Alone," The Virtual Team Builders Blog, October 6, 2010, *http://virtualteambuilders.wordpress.com/2010/10/06/employee-engagement-%E2%80%93-you-can%E2%80%99t-do-it-alone/*.

3. Ibid.

4. Bullock and Klein, op. cit.

5. All quotations in this case study are derived from a telephone interview conducted by Michael Savitt with Mark Hamberlin, Worldwide Leader, Global Staffing at Cisco, on August 22, 2011.

CHAPTER 3

1. Bureau of Labor Statistics, "American Time Use Survey—2010 Results," U.S. Department of Labor, Bureau of Labor Statistics, June 22, 2011, *www.bls.gov/news.release/atus.nr0.htm*.
2. Robert Half International and CareerBuilder.com, "Executive Summary: A Tale of Two Job Markets," *The EDGE Report*, September 2008, *www.rhi.com/External_Sites/downloads/RHI/PressReleases/EDGE_Report_08-2008.pdf*.
3. Brandi Armstrong, "A Telework Program for Your Small Business: The Why and the How," EzineArticles.com, December 6, 2007, *http://ezinearticles.com/?A-Telework-Program-For-Your-Small-Business—The-Why-And-The-How&id=869315*.
4. Chad Thompson and Pat Caputo, "The Reality of Virtual Work: Is Your Organization Ready?," Aon Consulting, 2009, *www.aon.com/usa/attachments/virtual_worker_whitepaper.pdf*.
5. Charles Bullock and Jennifer Tucker Klein, "Virtual Work Environments in the Post-Recession Era," Brandman University, 2011, *www.brandman.edu/pdf/virtual_teams_brandman_forrester_white_paper.pdf*.
6. All quotations in this Case Study are derived from an e-mail interview conducted by Michael Savitt with Heather Henshall, HR Project Coordinator, American Fidelity Assurance Company, on August 2, 2011.

CHAPTER 4

1. Emily Busch, Jenna Nash, and Bradford S. Bell, "Remote Work: An Examination of Current Trends and Emerging Issues," Spring 2011, Center for Advanced Human Resource Studies, Cornell University, *www.ilr.cornell.edu/cahrs/research/upload/Spring2011_CAHRSRemoteWorkReport.pdf*.

2. Karol Rose, *Work-Life Effectiveness: Bottom Line Strategies for Today's Workplace*, Scottsdale, Ariz.: WorldatWork Press, 2006.
3. Chris Young, "The Real Costs of Employee Turnover," The Rainmaker Group, February 6, 2007, *www.articlesbase.com/human-resources-articles/the-real-costs-of-employee-turnover-101420.html*.
4. James L. Heskett, Thomas O. Jones, Gary W. Loveman, W. Earl Sasser, Jr., and Leonard A. Schlesinger, "Putting the Service-Profit Chain to Work," *Harvard Business Review*, March–April 1994, *http://pagesetup.com/images/content/hbr-article.pdf*.
5. "Customer Service Facts," Customer Service Manager.com, *www.customerservicemanager.com/customer-service-facts.htm*.
6. Medtronic, "Total Employee Engagement," 2010 Corporate Citizenship Report, 2010, *www.medtronic.com/2010CitizenshipReport/total-employee/index.html*.
7. Laura Souza, "Kronos Global Absence Survey Shows Employees Around the World Playing Hooky With China Leading the Pack," Kronos, August 31, 2011, *www.kronos.com/pr/kronos-global-absence-survey-shows-employees-around-the-world-playing-hooky-with-china-leading-the-pack.aspx*.
8. "Absenteeism," SuiteCommute, *www.suitecommute.com/research-and-statistics/statistics/absenteeism/*.
9. Michael O'Brien, "What's Keeping You Up Now?" *Human Resource Executive*, September 2, 2011, *www.hreonline.com/HRE/story.jsp?storyId=533340817*.

CHAPTER 5

1. Albert Mehrabian, *Silent Messages*, Belmont, Calif.: Wadsworth, 1971.
2. HR Solutions' National Normative Database, *https://actionpro.hrsolutionsinc.com* (normative items).
3. E-mail interview by Michael Savitt with Sandy Burud, Principal, Flex Employment Services at FlexPaths, on August 18, 2011.

4. Microsoft Office, "Microsoft Home Office Makeover," Microsoft Office Fact Sheet, June 2007, *www.microsoft.com/presspass/presskits/2007office/docs/MSHomeOfficeFS.doc*.
5. All quotations are derived from a telephone interview conducted by Kevin Sheridan with Frits van Paasschen, president and chief executive officer of Starwood Hotels & Resorts Worldwide, on July 25th, 2011.
6. HR Solutions' National Normative Database, *https://actionpro.hrsolutionsinc.com* (normative items).

CHAPTER 6

1. Tatiana Morales, "Virtual Doctors: A Growing Trend," CBS News, February 11, 2009, *www.cbsnews.com/stories/2002/06/21/earlyshow/saturday/main513017.shtml*.
2. All quotations in this case study are derived from a telephone interview conducted by Michael Savitt with Steve Cadigan, vice president of people operations at LinkedIn, on August 25, 2011.
3. All quotations in this Case Study are derived from a telephone interview conducted by Michael Savitt with Lisa McGill, vice president of Human Resources at Brocade Communications Systems, Inc., on August 18, 2011.
4. Heinz Tschabitscher, "How Many Emails Are Sent Every Day?," About.com: Email, *http://email.about.com/od/emailtrivia/f/emails_per_day.htm*.
5. Toby Ward, "Employee Social Networking: Sabre Town Case Study," Prescient Digital Media, May 27, 2011, *www.prescientdigital.com/articles/intranet-articles/employee-social-networking-case-study*.
6. Lindsey Miller, "Employee Blog Connects Frontline Workers," Ragan's HR Communication, September 14, 2009, *www.hrcommunication.com/Main/Articles/Employee_blog_connects_frontline_workers_824.aspx*.
7. Jolie O'Dell, "Is Working From Home Becoming the Norm?," Mashable, April 5, 2011, *http://mashable.com/2011/04/05/wfh-survey/*.

8. Kenneth E. Fracaro, "The Consequences of Micromanaging," *Contract Management*, July 2007, 4–8, *www.ncmahq.org/files/Articles/ECBOA_CM0707_C01.pdf*.
9. "The Challenges of Working in Virtual Teams," RW3 CultureWizard, 2010, *http://rw-3.com/VTSReportv7.pdf*.

CHAPTER 7

1. Andrea Ozias, "Telework 2011," The Dieringer Research Group Inc. and WorldatWork, June 2011, *www.worldatwork.org/waw/adimLink?id=53034*.
2. All quotations in this Case Study are derived from an e-mail interview conducted by Michael Savitt with Aimée Eubanks Davis, Executive Vice President of People, Community, and Diversity at Teach For America, on August 9, 2011.
3. All quotations in this Case Study are derived from a telephone interview conducted by Michael Savitt with Mike A. McAlister, 1st Lieutenant, Communications Center at Fairfax County Police Department, on September 4, 2011.
4. All quotations in this Case Study are derived from a telephone interview conducted by Michael Savitt with Marc Davidson, Lieutenant, Basic Training Compliance Officer at Fairfax County Fire and Rescue Department, on August 30, 2011.
5. "Pros and Cons," Telework Research Network, *www.teleworkresearchnetwork.com/pros-cons*.
6. In-person interview conducted by Amelia Forczak with Phil Schreiber, Partner at Holland & Knight, on September 1, 2011.
7. Ibid.
8. (3)"ROWE Results," CultureRx, *www.gorowe.com/know-rowe/rowe-results/*.

FINAL THOUGHTS

1. All quotes in this chapter are derived from an e-mail interview conducted by Amelia Forczak with Jerry Linenger, retired United States Navy flight surgeon and NASA astronaut, on September 7, 2011.

INDEX

ABOUT THE AUTHOR

Kevin Sheridan is chief engagement officer and chief consultant of **HR Solutions** and directs all survey work conducted by the firm. He has extensive experience in the field, having co-founded three successful survey-related organizations. Having done consulting for some of the world's largest corporations, Mr. Sheridan has earned several distinctive awards and honors. One of his most notable recognitions was for the creation of HR360, which won *Human Resource Executive* magazine's "HR Product of the Year" award. His newest innovation, PEER, has recently been nominated for the same award.

Mr. Sheridan received a Master of business administration degree from the **Harvard Business School** in 1988, concentrating his degree in Managerial Decision-making and Strategy, human resources management, and organizational behavior. Prior to business school, Mr. Sheridan spent four years with **Chase Manhattan Bank, N.A.**, in New York City, London, and Japan. Mr. Sheridan then worked for **Goldman, Sachs & Co.**, while attending **Harvard**. After graduating from **Harvard**, Mr. Sheridan founded **Collegiate Research Services, Inc. (CRS)**. **CRS** was established for the sole purpose of introducing the **American Career and College Entry Service (ACCES)**. Featured in numerous publications, including *Business Week* and *USA Today*, **ACCES** used a survey to create the first electronic link between students and organizations to provide opportunities for further education and training.